CUTEST EVER
BABY TOYS
TO KNIT

CUTEST EVER
BABY TOYS
TO KNIT

OVER 20 ADORABLE PROJECTS

Val Pierce

TRAFALGAR SQUARE
North Pomfret, Vermont

First published in the United States of America in 2014 by
Trafalgar Square Books
North Pomfret, VT 05053

ISBN: 978-1-57076-709-8
Library of Congress Control Number: 2014936076

Publisher: Fiona Schultz
Editor: Simona Hill
Designer: Tracy Loughlin
Stylist: Sue Stubbs
Photographer: Sue Stubbs
Production director: Olga Dementiev

Printer: Toppan Leefung Printing Limited, China

10 9 8 7 6 5 4 3 2 1

Contents

Introduction

Everyone loves making toys for newborn babies and little people. These items are usually cute, bright and colorful and being small in scale, are generally quick to make. With all these requirements in mind I have designed 30 gifts and toys for you to make that are sure to delight the recipient as much as the project maker. From a cuddly penguin to a brightly colored starry face ball, a lovely friendly dinosaur to some sweet little booties, you are sure to find something in this volume to make for that special little person.

You will see that most toy patterns are usually knitted in either garter stitch or stockinette stitch using smaller needles than would normally be used for the weight of yarn. The reason for this is so that the resulting fabric will be of a more dense texture, be firmer to the touch and will not stretch too much when stuffed, and the stuffing shouldn't migrate through the fabric.

Choosing designs and yarns

Before you begin, it is very important to bear in mind the age of the child that you are making the project for. Babies and toddlers will constantly put things into their mouths to investigate them. These toys will need to be washed quite frequently so it's sensible to buy good quality wool that is machine washable.

The younger the child, the more basic and simple the toy needs to be. Bright bold colors, different textures and easy-to-hold shapes are perfect for tiny babies. The older the child then the more elaborate you can make the project.

When you have chosen the design you want to make, decide which yarn you might like to use. There are so many choices today, it will be quite a task to pick one. Although I have stated yarn weights for each project and specified the yarns I used to make these items it is possible to make almost every toy from oddments of the correct weight yarn from your stash.

Additionally the suggested yarn might not be available from your local yarn shop, or you may have yarn that you wish to use. Again, keep in mind the age of the child. Eyelash yarns and yarns with metallic threads running through them are fine for older children but the fibers may shed a little and therefore I would recommend testing them before using them to make gifts for babies.

Tips for sewing up your project

Having spent many hours knitting all the components needed to make the project, you will need to sew the pieces together. Take as much care sewing up the pieces as you would when making a garment; that way, arms and legs will be the same size, and the whole toy will be in proportion when it's finished. It is always better to count rows and fit like to like, so when you sew them together all the rows will match.

Fabrics can be stitched together using more than one method. Garter stitch is much neater sewn on the right sides of the fabric. Arranging the pieces flat and side by side, you can match row for row by sewing through the "little bumps" of the garter stitch alternately, then pulling the yarn quite firmly to draw the pieces together. This gives a neat, flat and almost invisible join. You will find it much easier to see what you are doing when the right sides of the fabric are facing you, too. You can also join stockinette stitch in a similar way, but this time sewing through between the "V" made by a stitch and picking up the horizontal loop in the center of it. You will work picking up the stitch alternately on adjacent sides of the fabric, then drawing the work together quite tightly. This gives an invisible seam and allows you to match stripes and patterns really easily. A third method used is back stitch. This is worked on the inside of the fabric, and gives a small neat ridge; it is more bulky than the other two methods of seaming but it can be very strong and is a good option when you need strength adding to a particular join.

Tips for stuffing your project

Novice toy makers are often quite nervous about stuffing their toys, fearing that they may spoil them. Most toy parts will need to be stuffed quite firmly so that they hold their shape. Do this by adding a small amount of stuffing at a time and pushing it well into the base of the part you are working on. I always tease out each piece as I use it, that way it is more pliable and more likely to achieve a smooth shape. Always try to stuff each part equally, so check legs and arms against each other as you work to make sure that they match. Don't over-stuff pieces since you need to be able to sew limbs to the body and if they are full to the brim then there will be no spare fabric to use. Hands and feet will need extra stuffing and shaping.

Heads need to be shaped to give the best possible result. Look at the photograph as you work to check the shape and see where extra stuffing may be needed. Take care and work slowly. Check frequently that the head isn't becoming too big for the body and vice versa. The toy needs to be stable and not top heavy. You can shape and stuff as you work, pushing more into some areas such as cheeks and noses and less into others. Don't sew on any facial features until you are satisfied with the shape of the head. Loosely tack (baste) the head to the body to see how it sits in proportion to the rest of the toy. You can always take out or add more stuffing at this stage. Only when you are completely satisfied should you sew the head to the body. To avoid a wobbly head, a result of the head and body not being equally stuffed, add a little more stuffing or remove a little by opening a tiny part of a seam. First catch the head to the body with a few stitches around the neck. This will hold it steady while you sew the two pieces more firmly together. Check all the time that the head is straight, not too far back or too far forward. Mostly heads face forward and are straight. Angling the head very slightly can add a cute look.

Before stitching the arms and legs to a toy check that they are stuffed equally and that the shaping matches. Pin the limbs into position before you sew them in place. Try to get equal distances between the pieces and check whether your toy needs to be sitting or standing.

Using matching yarn and a blunt-ended needle, use any long tail ends from the casting on or off, for sewing up the pieces. Sew the limbs onto the body very firmly, taking a stitch on the limb and then a stitch on the body alternately until you have sewn it firmly in place. Go over the same area twice if you are unsure whether the stitching is firm enough.

Adding facial and other features

Adding features is the *pièce de résistance* and can make or break the success of the look of your toy. It takes practice to get features looking just right so try out your techniques on a spare piece of fabric before you begin. Look at the photograph of the face you are going to copy. Note the placement of the eyes and nose and mouth. Put markers on the face in the areas where those features will go before you begin. Safety eyes need to be added when the head is partially stuffed. Once they are locked in place you can't remove and reposition them. Push the eye through the fabric in the desired position, then push the washer onto the back of the eye; it will "click" when it is correctly placed. When embroidering features you can, of course, unpick and re-embroider them, if needed.

There are many ways of adding embroidered features. Most noses for larger animals can be stitched with straight stitches placed quite close together so that they form a dense mass. Using wool or embroidery thread and a blunt-ended needle, work consecutive lines in close parallel to each other. It is easy to pull the yarn too tightly when doing this so work evenly and slowly to achieve a good result. Pulling too tightly will result in a puckered piece of fabric and an odd-shaped nose. Eyes can be embroidered using French knots. If you keep the tension even for each eye, you can add shape to the face. Their positon can also help to depict the nose too. Practice is the only way to achieve good results, but patience is needed too. So, if you get it wrong the first time, then unpick and start again. You will be glad you did when you see your finished toy.

Knitting abbreviations

Alt = alternate

Beg = beginning

Cm =centimeters

CO =cast on

Foll = following

Garter stitch = every row knit

In = inches

Inc = increase

K = knit

K2tog = knit two stitches together

K2tog tbl = knit two stitches together through the back loop

P = purl

Patt = pattern

Psso = pass slipped stitch over

Rem = remain

Rep = repeat

RS = right side

Skpso = sl 1, K1, pass slipped stitch over

St = stitch

Stockinette stitch = alternating knit and purl rows

WS = wrong side

Yo = yarn over

Crochet abbreviations

Ch = chain

Dc = double crochet (UK: treble)

Sc2tog = work the next 2 sc together to decrease a stitch

Hdc = half double crochet (UK: half treble)

Sc = single crochet (UK: double crochet)

Sl st = slipped stitch

US and UK terminology

Bind off	=	Cast off
Seed stitch	=	Moss stitch
Stockinette stitch	=	Stocking stitch
Yarn over	=	Yarn forward

Knitting needle conversion chart

US	UK	Metric
0	14	2 mm
1	13	2.25 mm
2	12	2.75 mm
–	11	3 mm
3	10	3.25 mm
4	–	3.5 mm
5	9	3.75 mm
6	8	4 mm
7	7	4.5 mm
8	6	5 mm
9	5	5.5 mm
10	4	6 mm

Crochet hook conversion chart

US	UK	Metric
–	14	2 mm
B/1	13	2.25
–	12	2.5
C/2	–	2.75
–	11	3
D/3	10	3.25
E/4	9	3.5
F/5	–	3.75
G/6	8	4
7	7	4.5
H/8	6	5
I/9	5	5.5
J/10	4	6

Great Big Dinosaur

Little boys and girls will love this dinosaur buddy. He is easy to carry around with his long neck and is just waiting for hugs. Making the toy will take time and patience but is well worth the effort. I have used felt to make the eyes, but you can easily embroider them, if you prefer.

✳✳✳ Experienced

You will need
2 x 2 oz (50 g) balls Patons Fairytale Dreamtime DK
 random-dyed, shade 4971 (A)
2 x 2 oz (50 g) balls Patons Fairytale Dreamtime DK
 Lime Green, shade 4952 (B)
1 x 2 oz (50 g) ball Patons Fairytale Dreamtime DK
 Orange, shade 4951 (C)
Scraps of black and white felt, for the eyes
US 5 (UK 9, 3.75 mm) knitting needles
Polyester fiberfill
Tapestry needle, for sewing up
Sewing kit

Gauge
Is not critical on this project.

Dinosaur
Using Yarn A, CO 16 sts.
Row 1: Purl.
Row 2: Inc knitwise into every stitch (32 sts).
Beg with a purl row, work 22 rows St st.
Row 25: (K2tog 6 times), inc in each of next 8 sts,
(K2tog 6 times) (28 sts).
Inc 1 st at each end of next and every foll 4th row until
there are 38 sts.
Work 7 rows St st.
Next row: Inc knitwise in each st to end (76 sts).
Work 30 rows St st.
Next row: (K2, K2tog) to end.
Work 14 rows St st.
Next row: (K1, K2tog) to end.
Work 9 rows St st.
Dec 1 st at each end of next and every alt row until

4 sts remain. Bind off. This is the tail end.

Spots
Make 8
Using Yarn C, CO 3 sts.
Row 1: Knit.
Row 2: Inc in first and last stitch.
Knit 3 rows.
Dec 1 st at each end of next row.
Row 7: Knit.
Row 8: Sl 1, K2tog, psso. Finish off.

Back Plates
Make 8
Using Yarn B, CO 2 sts.
Row 1: Knit.
Row 2: Inc in each st (4 sts).
Row 3: Knit.
Row 4: Inc in first stitch, knit to last st, inc.
Cont as for rows 3 and 4 until there are 12 sts on the needle. Slip the sts onto a spare needle. Make 7 more plates in the same way.
Now work across all the plates, slipping each off the spare needle and onto the knitting needle (96 sts).
Knit 2 rows. Bind off.

Legs
Make 4
Using Yarn A, CO 18 sts.
Row 1: Purl.
Row 2: Inc knitwise into each stitch to end of row (36 sts).
Work 8 rows St st on these rows.
Row 11: K8, (K2tog 10 times), K8 (26 sts).
Work 13 rows St st beg with a purl row.
Row 25: K6, (K2tog 3 times), K2, (K2tog

3 times), K6.
Row 26: Purl.
Bind off.

Assembling the Dinosaur
Sew in all loose ends. Fold in half, right sides together, so that the body seam runs underneath the dinosaur. Stitch seam firmly, leaving the head and tail ends open for stuffing. Turn right sides out and stuff the shape, working from each end, adding a little at a time, and pushing the stuffing into place with the blunt end of the knitting needle. Work slowly and fill firmly. When you are happy with the shape, secure the nose and tail openings.

Cut shapes from felt for the eyes and sew in place on the head, or embroider them, if you prefer.

Embroider the nostrils and smiley mouth with black yarn. Sew the spots on in a random pattern.

Pin the plates in place along the back of the dinosaur, sew firmly on each side to make them stand up.

Sew up the leg seams, leaving the tops open, and stuff firmly. Attach the legs to the dinosaur, making sure they are level so that he will stand on a flat surface.

Halloween Booties

These super-cute little orange booties will be so fun for Baby to wear on Halloween, though you could change the colors to suit your own special occasion. Use all one shade of yarn or mix and match whatever colors you have in your stash.

❋ Beginner

You will need

1 x 2 oz (50 g) ball Patons Fairytale Dreamtime DK
   Orange, shade 4951
1 x 2 oz (50 g) ball Patons Fairytale Dreamtime DK
   Lime Green, shade 4952
1 m (1 yd) narrow matching green ribbon
2 orange flower buttons
US 6 (UK 8, 4 mm) knitting needles
Tapestry needle, for sewing up
Sewing kit

Gauge

22 sts x 30 rows St st measure 4 in (10 cm) using
US 6 (UK 8, 4 mm) needles.

Size

To fit baby 3–6 months

Special abbreviations

M1 = Make 1 stitch by picking up the strand between
   the stitch you have just knitted and the next stitch
   on the needle, then knitting into the back of it.

Booties

Make 2

Using Orange yarn, CO 27 sts.

Knit 1 row.

Row 2: K2 (M1, K11, M1, K1) twice, K1 (31 sts).

Row 3 and following alternate rows: Knit.

Row 5: K2, M1, K12, M1, K3, M1, K12, M1, K2 (35 sts).

Row 7: K2, M1, K13, M1, K5, M1, K13, M1, K2 (39 sts).

Row 9: K2, M1, K14, M1, K7, M1, K14, M1, K2 (43 sts).

Change to Lime Green and work 6 rows St st. Break yarn. (These 6 rows will be folded in half and sewn together to form the ridge around the base of the bootie.)

Join in Orange and work 12 rows garter st.

Shape instep

Next row: K26, turn.

Next row: K9, turn.

Next row: K8, K2tog, turn.

Next row: K8, K2tog tbl, turn.

Rep last two rows 5 times more, turn.

Next row: K9, knit across rem sts on the left-hand needle.

Next row: Knit across all sts (31 sts).

Work 2 rows in garter st.

Make eyelets: K2, *yo, K2tog, K1*, rep from * to * to last 2 sts, yo, K2tog.

Next row: Knit.

Change to Lime Green.

Knit 4 rows.

Next row: Purl.

Next row: Knit.

Next row: Knit.

Next row: Purl.

Next row: Knit.

Next row: Knit.

Next row: Purl.

Next row: Knit.

Next row: Knit.

Next row: Purl. Break off.

Join Orange yarn and knit 4 rows. Bind off.

Assembling the booties

Fold the six green rows of St st in half onto the right side of the work. Working from the wrong side of the bootie, catch the corresponding stitches from the top and bottom of the rows to hold the ridge together. Sew the foot and back seams on the booties.

Cut the ribbon in half and thread a piece through the eyelet holes on each bootie and tie in a bow. Sew a button to the front of each bootie.

Daisy the Baby Dinosaur

Every little one loves a cuddly dino to take around with them. This one is very simple and quick to make. Use bright or pastel colors. Let your imagination run wild and create a special toy for a favorite little person.

✲✲ Intermediate

You will need

1 x 2 oz (50 g) ball Patons Fairytale Dreamtime DK
   yarn in Strawberry, shade 04953 (S)
1 x 2 oz (50 g) ball Patons Fairytale Dreamtime DK
   yarn in Aqua, shade 04957 (A)
Oddments of pale blue, white and green, for the
   embroidery
Black yarn, for the features
US 5 (UK 9, 3.75 mm) knitting needles
Polyester fiberfill
Tapestry needle, for sewing up
Sewing kit

Gauge

22 sts x 30 rows St st = 4 in (10 cm).

Size

Length 12 in (30 cm) from tip of tail to nose

Dinosaur

BODY
Using Yarn S, CO 15 sts.
Row 1: Purl.
Row 2: Inc knitwise in each st to end (30 sts).
Now work in St st for 5 rows.
Row 8–13: Cont in St st and inc 1 st at each end of next 6 rows (42 sts).
Row 14: (K2tog 6 times), K18, (K2tog 6 times) (30 sts).
Work 5 rows in St st.
Row 20: K8, inc in every st to last 8 sts, K8 (44 sts).
Work 17 rows St st.
Row 38: (K2, K2tog) to end of row (33 sts).
Work 9 rows St st.

Row 48: (K1, K2tog) to end of row (22 sts).
Work 9 rows St st.
Row 58: K2tog across row (11 sts).
Work 11 rows St st.
Row 70: K2tog across row to last st, K1 (6 sts).
Break yarn and thread through rem sts, pull up tight
and finish off. This is the tail end.

Collar
Using Yarn A, CO 30 sts.
Purl 1 row.
Row 2: K1, inc in each st to last st, K1.
Work 9 rows St st.
Row 12: Using S, K1, *yo, sl 1, K1, psso*, rep from * to
* to last st, K1.
Row 13: Purl. Break off S and continue in A.
Work 8 rows St st.
Row 22: K2tog across row. Bind off.

Legs
Make 4
Using Yarn S, CO 10 sts.
Row 1: Knit.
Row 2: Inc in each st to end (20 sts).
Work 5 rows St st.
Row 8 (Dec row): K5, (K2tog 5 times), K5.
Knit 9 rows. Bind off.

Horns
Make 2
Using Yarn A, CO 10 sts.
Work 8 rows St st.
Row 9: K1, K2tog tbl, K4, K2tog, K1.
Row 10: Purl.
Row 11: K1, K2tog tbl, K2, K2tog, K1.
Row 12: Purl.

Row 13: K1, K2tog tbl, K2tog, K1.
Row 14: P2tog twice.
K2tog. Finish off.

Assembling the dinosaur

Work in all ends on all pieces. Sew seam of main body;
this will run on the underside. Leave the nose end
open; stuff a little at a time to make a firm shape. Sew
the end of the nose together with a flat seam. Sew
side and foot seam on legs, stuff firmly. Attach to the
body, making sure they are level. Fold the collar in half
and stitch the side seams. The pink line on the collar
will face the front. Sew seams on horns and lightly
stuff. Stitch in place on the front of the head. Place the
collar around the neck and slightly sloping forward.
Stitch in place.
Using contrast yarns, embroider French knots all over
the back of the dinosaur. Embroider the nostrils and
mouth with black yarn. Cut out felt shapes for the
eyes, glue first and then oversew in place or, if you
prefer, embroider the eyes onto the face.

Soft and Squishy Playbook

Using pretty yarns from your stash, create a soft playbook for Baby. Each page has a knitted and embroidered picture, and the use of plenty of bright shades of yarn adds appeal for little minds. Ensure that every design is securely stitched in place.

❋ Beginner

You will need

1 x 2 oz (50 g) ball Sirdar Snuggly Tiny Tots DK Crystal Blue, shade 976

1 x 2 oz (50 g) ball Sirdar Snuggly Baby Speckle DK Herbie Green, shade 122

1 x 2 oz (50 g) ball Sirdar Snuggly Baby Speckle DK Jollie Mollie (lilac), shade 125

1 x 2 oz (50 g) ball Sirdar Snuggly Baby Speckle DK Lemon, shade 252

Oddments of DK yarn in lots of colors for the appliqué and embroidery

US 6 (UK 8, 4 mm) knitting needles

Fabric bow, for the teddy

Gauge

Is not critical for this project.

Book

PAGES

Make 4, one in each of the main colors

Using color of your choice, CO 28 sts.

Knit 6 rows garter st (every row knit).

Change to St st with a garter st border as follows:

Row 1: Knit.

Row 2: K5, P to last 5 sts, K5.

Work another 32 rows as set.

Now work 8 rows in garter st, changing color if you like.

Change to St st with a garter st border (as set for rows 1 and 2) for another 34 rows.

Change to garter st and work 8 more rows. Bind off.

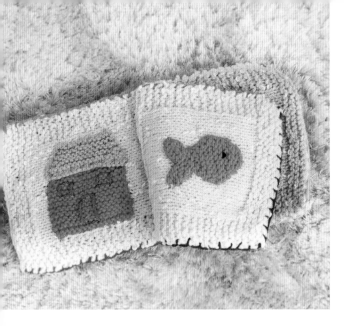

a smiley face. Take outer edge and sew around the yellow circle. Join the two ends together.

House
Using Crystal Blue, CO 16 sts.
Cont in garter st for 24 rows. Bind off.

Roof
Using Herbie Green, CO 18 sts.
Knit 2 rows.
Dec 1 st at each end of the row on the next and foll alt rows until there are 10 sts. Bind off.
Place roof onto top edge of house and sew in place.
Embroider windows and doors. Sew firmly to page.

Fish
Using orange, CO 2 sts.
Knit 1 row.
Row 2: Inc in both sts (4 sts).
Row 3: Knit.
Row 4: Inc in first st, K to last st, inc (6 sts).
Cont as set for rows 3 and 4 until there are 10 sts.
Work 6 rows garter st.
Next row: K2tog, work to last 2 sts, K2tog.
Next row: Knit.
Rep last 2 rows until 4 sts remain.
Work 2 rows on these sts.
Next row: Inc in next st, K to last st, inc.
Repeat last row until there are 14 sts.
Knit 1 row and bind off. Thread some spare yarn onto a tapestry needle and pull in the center of the tail slightly to give shape. Sew the fish onto the center of the page. Embroider an eye.

Sun
Using Lemon, CO 8 sts.
Knit 2 rows.
Inc at each end of next and following alt rows until there are 16 sts.
Knit 6 rows straight.
Dec 1 st at each end of next and following alt rows until there are 8 sts.
Knit 2 rows and bind off.

Sun's outer edge
Using a random stripe yarn, CO 5 sts.
Rows 1 and 2: Knit.
Row 3: Bind off 3 sts. K to end.
Row 4: Knit.
Row 5: CO 3 sts. K to end.
Repeat last 5 rows until piece, when slightly stretched, fits all around the outside edge of the sun. Bind off.
Sew main part of sun to page, embroider eyes and

Teddy

Using brown, CO 9 sts.

Row 1: Inc in first st, knit to last st, inc.

Row 2: Purl.

Rep last 2 rows until there are 15 sts.

Work 4 rows St st.

Next row: K2tog, K to last 2 sts, K2tog.

Next row: Purl.

Repeat last 2 sts until there are 7 sts, ending with a purl st. Bind off.

Muzzle

Using brown, CO 3 sts.

Working in garter st throughout:

Knit 2 rows.

Row 3: Inc in each st to end (6 sts).

Row 4: Knit.

Row 5: Inc in first and last st (8 sts).

Knit 4 rows.

Row 10: K2tog at each end.

Row 11: Knit.

Row 12: K2tog at each end.

Row 13: Knit.

Row 14: K2tog twice. Bind off.

Ears

Make 2

Using brown, CO 4 sts.

Knit 2 rows.

Row 3: Inc in first and last sts (6 sts).

Knit 4 rows.

Row 8: K2tog at each end of row.

Row 9: Knit.

Row 10: K2tog twice.

Row 11: K2tog. Bind off.

Sew muzzle onto lower center of face and stuff lightly to give shape. Sew the ears on to each side of the head, gathering at the top a little to give shape. Embroider the features. Firmly sew a bow to the top of the head. Position the teddy on the page and stitch in place.

Car

Body
Using your choice of color, CO 20 sts.
Work 10 rows St st.
Bind off 10 sts. Knit to end.
Next row: Purl.
Work 4 more rows St st.
Next row: K2tog at each end of row.
Next row: Purl.
Next row: K2tog at each end of row. Bind off.

Wheels
Make 2
Using black, CO 4 sts.
Knit 2 rows.
Row 3: Inc at each end of row (6 sts).
Knit 4 rows.
Row 8: K2tog at each end of row.
Knit 2 rows. Bind off.

Window
Using white, CO 8 sts.
Work in St st for 8 rows ending with a purl row. Bind off.
Sew the window and wheels onto the body of the car.
Embroider the triangular corner window.
Firmly sew the car to the page.

Boat
Using dark blue, CO 8 sts.
Working in garter st, knit 2 rows.
Inc 2 sts at each end of next and foll alt rows until there are 20 sts.
Knit 1 row and bind off.

Large sail
Using white, CO 12 sts.
Work 4 rows St st.
Row 5: Knit to last 2 sts, K2tog tbl.
Row 6: Purl.
Row 7: Knit.
Row 8: Purl.
Row 9: Knit to last 2 sts, K2tog tbl.
Row 10: Purl.
Repeat last 2 rows until all sts are worked off. Finish off.

Small sail
Using white, CO 10 sts.
Work 4 rows in St st.
Row 5: K2tog, knit to end.
Row 6: Purl.
Work 2 rows in St st.
Row 9: K2tog, knit to end.
Row 10: Purl.
Rep last 2 rows until all sts are worked off. Finish off.
Arrange the pieces of the boat on the page, pin, then stitch securely in place. Embroider the mast in brown. Embroider a stripe along the base of the boat. Using red, make a flag using a few straight stitches.

Flower

Petals
Make 5
Using pink, CO 2 sts.
Knit 1 row.
Row 2: Inc in both sts (4 sts).
Row 3: Knit.
Row 4: Inc in first st, knit to last st, inc (8 sts).
Knit 4 rows.
Row 9: K2tog, knit to last 2 sts, k2tog.

Row 10: Knit to end.
Repeat last 2 rows until there are 4 sts.
Next row: K2tog twice.
Next row: K2tog. Finish off.
Arrange the petals in a circle on the page, then pin
and sew in place. Embroider a large French knot in the
flower center. Embroider a couple of leaves at one side
of the flower.

SNAIL
Shell
Using random stripe yarn, CO 56 sts.
Knit 1 row.
Row 2: *Bind off 1 st in the normal way, yarn round
needle, bind that st off,* rep from * to * all across row.
The piece will curl up as you work.

Body
Using orange, CO 40 sts.
Work 10 rows in garter st. Bind off.
Coil the shell into a circle, tweaking the shape a little
as you go. Stitch in place.
Fold the body in half lengthways and stitch into a
sausage. Form the piece into a body and head. Sew in
place. Embroider eyes on top of the head.

Assembling the book

Tidy all the thread ends. Put two pages tog wrong sides
facing, then, using a length of bright yarn threaded
through a tapestry needle, sew the pages tog using
blanket stitch. Repeat with the other two pages. Use
different colors for each side of the pages to make
the book look really bright and interesting. Using a
matching yarn, sew through the center of the pages to
hold them together. Make a twisted cord and thread
it through the spine of the book; tie the ends in a

bow. Sew the motifs onto each page, ensuring that
everything is stitched very firmly. Inquisitive little
hands are adept at removing bits and pieces, which
could form a health and safety hazard if not properly
secure. Never leave Baby unattended when playing
with anything attached to cords.

Starry Face Ball

Even the youngest baby will enjoy holding this pretty, soft ball. With its colorful appearance and multi-colored starry faces it is sure to please. You can also help a toddler to develop co-ordination, by teaching them to roll the ball in a specific direction and to play catch, since the ball is completely safe for indoor use.

✳ Beginner

You will need
Oddments of 8 different colored DK yarns
US 5 (UK 9, 3.75 mm) knitting needles
Polyester fiberfill
Tapestry needle, for sewing up
Sewing kit

Size
Circumference measures 18 in (46 cm).

Ball
The ball is worked in one piece, with each of the eight sections knitted using a different color yarn.

Using color of your choice, CO 34 sts.
Row 1: Knit.
**Row 2: Sl 1, knit to last st, turn.
Rows 3 and 4: Sl 1, knit to last 2 sts, turn.
Rows 5 and 6: Sl 1, knit to last 3 sts, turn.
Continue as set, working 1 less stitch at the end of every row until 8 sts remain unworked at each end.
Next row: Sl 1, knit to last 9 sts, turn.
Next 2 rows: Sl 1, knit across all stitches firmly.**
Break yarn and join in next color.
Row 1: Knit.
Now work from ** to **.
Cont working sections in different colors until all

8 sections are complete. Bind off.

STARRY FACES
Make 6
Using color of your choice, CO 55 sts.
Row 1: Knit.
Row 2: K4, sl 1, K2tog, psso, *K8, sl 1, K2tog, psso*, rep from * to * to last 4 sts, K4.
Row 3: K3, sl 1, K2tog, psso, *K6, sl 1, K2tog, psso*, rep from * to * to last 3 sts, K3.

Row 4: K2, sl 1, K2tog, psso, *K4, sl 1, K2tog, psso*, rep from * to * to last 2 sts, K2.
Row 5: K1, sl 1, K2tog, psso, *K2, sl 1, K2tog, psso*, rep from * to * to last st, K1.
Row 6: *Sl 1, K2tog, psso*, rep from * to * to end (5 sts).
Break yarn and run thread through rem sts, draw up tightly and secure. Stitch side seam of face. Using black yarn, stitch a smiley face.

Assembling the ball
Work in all ends. Run a gathering thread around each end of the ball and draw up tightly. Join seam neatly, leaving a space to stuff. Stuff firmly and make a firm, round shape. Stitch up the remaining opening. Securely sew the stars onto the ball in random positions.

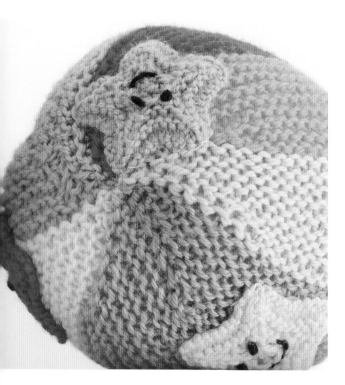

Oscar the Spotty Dog

With his cute face and eye-catching spotty markings, this little puppy is looking for a new owner. Oscar is quite easy to knit. Use my color choice or create your own using remnants from your stash. Add more or fewer spots to his body as the whim takes you.

✳✳ Intermediate

You will need
2 x 2 oz (50 g) balls Sirdar Snuggly DK White, shade 251
1 x 2 oz (50 g) ball Sirdar Snuggly DK Baby Grey, shade 427
Oddment of red DK, for the collar
US 6 (UK 8, 5 mm) knitting needles
US 5 (UK 9, 3.75 mm) knitting needles
Polyester fiberfill
Tapestry needle, for sewing up
Sewing kit

Gauge
Is not critical on this project.

Size
9 in (23 cm) sitting

Dog
HEAD
Using US 6 (UK 8, 4 mm) knitting needles and White, CO 6 sts.
Row 1: Purl.
Row 2: Inc in each st (12 sts).
Row 3: Purl.
Row 4: Inc in each st (24 sts).
Row 5: Purl.
Row 6: *K1, inc in next st*, rep from * to * to end (36 sts).
Row 7: Purl.
Work 20 rows in St st, mark this line for the nose. Work another 12 rows St st.
Next row: K2tog across row.
Beg with a purl row, work 3 rows St st.

Next row: K2tog across row.
Do not bind off; run yarn through sts on needles, draw up tight and finish off.

Body

Using US 6 (UK 8, 4 mm) knitting needles and White, CO 10 sts.
Work 2 rows St st.
Row 3: Inc in every st (20 sts).
Beg with a purl row, work 3 rows St st.
Row 7: *Inc in next st, K1*, rep from * to * to end (30 sts).
Beg with a purl row, work 5 rows St st.
Row 13: *K2, inc in next st*, rep from * to * to end (40 sts).
Beg with a purl row, work 5 rows St st.
Row 19: *K3, inc in next st*, rep from * to * to end (50 sts).
Beg with a purl row, work 7 rows St st.
Row 27: *K3, K2tog*, rep from * to * to end.
Row 28: Purl.
Work 4 rows St st.
Row 33: *K2, K2tog*, rep from * to * to end.
Row 34: Purl.
Work 8 rows St st.
Row 43: *K1, K2tog*, rep from * to * to end.
Row 44: Purl.
Work 4 rows St st.
Row 49: *K1, K2tog*, rep from * to * to last 2 sts, K2.
Row 50: Purl.
Row 51: K2tog across row. Bind off.
Finish off. This is the neck edge.

Arms
Make 2

Using US 6 (UK 8, 4 mm) knitting needles and White, CO 14 sts.
Work 2 rows St st.
Inc 1 st at each end of the next and foll alt rows until there are 24 sts.
Work 13 rows St st.
Next row: *Inc in next st, K2*, rep from * to * to end (32 sts).
Work 9 rows St st.
Next row: *K2tog, K2*, rep from * to * to end (24 sts).
Next row: Purl.
Next row: K2tog across row (12 sts).
Next row: Purl.
Next row: K2tog across row (6 sts).
Bind off.

Leg
Make 2
Using US 6 (UK 8, 4 mm) knitting needles and White, CO 14 sts.
Work 2 rows St st.
Inc 1 st at each end of next and foll alt rows until there are 26 sts, ending on a knit row.
Work 15 rows St st.
Next row: *K2, inc in next st*, rep from * to * to last 2 sts, K2 (34 sts) (mark this line with a contrast thread to gather for paws).
Work 9 rows St st.
Next row: *K2tog, K2*, rep from * to * to end (26 sts).
Next row: Purl.
Next row: K2tog to end (13 sts).
Next row: Purl.
Next row: K1, *K2tog*, rep from * to * to end (7 sts).
Bind off.

Ears

Make 2

Using US 6 (UK 8, 4 mm) knitting needles and Baby Grey, CO 9 sts.

Knit 1 row.

Working in garter st throughout, inc 1 st at each end of every row until there are 13 sts.

Next work 6 rows straight in garter st.

Next row: K1, *K2tog*, rep from * to * across row.

Bind off.

Nose

Using US 6 (UK 8, 4 mm) knitting needles and Baby Grey, CO 8 sts.

Work 4 rows St st.

K2tog at each end of next and foll alt rows until 2 sts remain, K2tog. Finish off.

Tail

Using US 6 (UK 8, 4 mm) knitting needles and White, CO 12 sts.

Work 14 rows St st.

Break white yarn and join in Baby Grey.

Work 2 rows St st.

Row 17: Dec 1 st at each end of next and foll alt rows until 2 sts rem, K2tog. Finish off.

Small spots

Make as many spots as you like

Using US 5 (UK 9, 3.75 mm) knitting needles and Baby Grey, CO 3 sts.

Row 1: Inc in first st, knit to last st, inc.

Knit 3 rows.

Row 5: Dec 1 st each end of row.

Row 6: Knit.

Row 7: Sl 1, K2tog, psso. Finish off.

Medium spots

Make as many spots as you like

Using US 5 (UK 9, 3.75 mm) knitting needles and Baby Grey, CO 5 sts.

Row 1: Knit.

Row 2: Inc in first and last st.

Knit 5 rows.

Next row: Dec 1 st at each end of next and foll alt row.

Next row: Knit.

Next row: Sl 1, K2tog, psso. Finish off.

Large Spots

Make as many spots as you like

Using US 5 (UK 9, 3.75 mm) knitting needles and Baby Grey, CO 7 sts.

Row 1: Knit.

Row 2: Inc in first and last st.

Knit 7 rows.

Dec 1 st at each end of next and 2 foll alt rows.

Next row: Knit.

Next row: Sl 1, K2tog, psso. Finish off.

Collar

Using red and US 6 (UK 8, 4 mm) knitting needles, CO 41 sts.

Row 1: K1, P1, across row to last st, K1.

Repeat last row 3 times more. Bind off.

Assembling the dog

Sew in all ends. The seam of the head runs along the underside. Fold the work in half and sew the seam, leaving a small opening at one end to allow stuffing. Stuff quite firmly and shape as you work. Close and secure. Thread a blunt-ended needle with cream yarn and run the needle in and out of every stitch on the marked row, beg and ending at the seam. Pull the yarn quite firmly to give shape to the nose, secure the thread ends and tie off. Sew the black nose patch in place and pad out slightly. Using the picture as a guide, embroider the features. Sew French knots onto each side of the muzzle. Pin the ears in position on each side of the head and sew in place. Turn the tops of the ears forward slightly. The body seam runs up the center back. Fold the body in half and sew seam as before, leaving an opening for stuffing. Stuff firmly and shape, then sew the opening closed. Sew the head to the body. Fold the tail in half and sew the seam, stuff lightly to give shape. Attach the tail to the back of the dog. Sew the arm and leg seams in the same way. Run a gathering thread around the base of the arms and legs at the marked rows, as for the nose, draw up firmly and secure. Attach the arms and legs to the body, remembering to place the legs so that the dog is in a sitting position and the seams are on the underside. Sew spots onto the head, body and arms in a random pattern. Sew the collar around the neck with the join at the center back.

Goody Two Shoes

Create these delightful little shoes for a newborn baby in just a couple of evenings.

They are worked mostly in garter stitch so a novice knitter can attempt them. I have

used two matching yarns but you can make them in just one color, if you prefer. Make

sure that you attach the pompoms very securely to the fronts of the shoes.

❄ Beginner

You will need
1 x 2 oz (50 g) ball Patons Fairytale Soft DK, Baby Blue,
   shade 6310 (A)
1 x 2 oz (50 g) ball Patons Fairytale Dreamtime DK
   blue/pink/yellow mix, shade 4970 (B)
US 3 (UK 10, 3.25 mm) knitting needles
2 small buttons
Tapestry needle, for sewing up
Sewing kit

Size
To fit birth to 3 months

Special abbreviations
M1 = make 1 stitch as follows: pick up and knit the
   strand that lies between the stitch you are knitting
   and the next stitch, and knit into the back of it.

Left shoe

Using Yarn A, CO 33 stitches.

Row 1: Knit.

Row 2: K1, M1, K15, M1, K1, M1, K15, M1, K1 (37 sts).

Row 3: Knit.

Row 4: K2, M1, K16, M1, K3, M1, K16, M1, K2 (41 sts).

Row 5: Knit.

Row 6: K3, M1, K14, M1, K5, M1, K14, M1, K3 (45 sts).

Row 7: Knit.

Row 8: K4, M1, K14, M1, K7, M1, K14, M1, K4 (49 sts).

*Change to Yarn B and work 4 rows St st.

Row 13 (Picot row): K1, *yo, K2tog*, rep from * to * to end.

Row 14: Purl.

Row 15: Knit

Row 16: Purl.*

Change to Yarn A and work 14 rows garter st. Change to Yarn B.

Row 31: K16, (sl 1, K1, psso 4 times), K1, (K2tog 4 times), K16 (41 sts).

Row 32: Knit.

Row 33: K10, bind off 21 sts, knit to end. ***

Slip first set of 10 stitches on holder.

Knit 3 rows and bind off.

Rejoin yarn where you started binding off 21 sts. CO 13 sts.

Next row: Knit across cast-on sts and 10 sts from holder (23 sts).

Next row (Buttonhole row): K18, K2tog, yo, K1 (21 sts).

Next row: Knit. Bind off.

Right shoe

Work as for left shoe to ***. Put first set of 10 sts on holder.

Next row: K10 sts on needle; turn work and CO 13 sts at end of row.

Next row: Knit.

Next row (Buttonhole row): K19, yo, K2tog, K1.

Next row: Knit.

Bind off all stitches on needle. Rejoin yarn to stitches on holder.

Knit 3 rows. Bind off.

Assembling the shoes

Thread a tapestry needle with a length of variegated yarn and a needle. With wrong sides facing, fold the picot edge rows from * to *, and sew together, matching stitch for stitch all along the row, to form a neat picot edging on the right side of the work. Sew the foot and back of the shoe. Sew buttons on to correspond with buttonholes. Using variegated yarn, make two tiny pompoms and sew very firmly to the front of each shoe.

Little Bunny Bag

What little girl wouldn't like to keep her special treasures in this cute little bag? It's so simple to make using stockinette and garter stitches. The bunny is knitted in pieces and sewn into place on the bag. Add a sparkly butterfly motif to the bunny's hair to complete the project.

❋ Beginner

You will need
1 x 2 oz (50 g) ball Sirdar Snuggly Tiny Tots DK Tweedy
   Plum, shade 912
1 x 2 oz (50 g) ball Bergere de France Plume, cream
   (This is a fluffy yarn that knits to aran weight.)
Oddments of black and brown DK, for the embroidery
US 7 (UK 7, 4.5 mm) knitting needles
Butterfly motif
Small button
Polyester fiberfill
Tapestry needle, for sewing up
Sewing kit

Gauge
Is not crucial on this project.

Size
7 x 5½ in (18 x 14 cm)

Bag
Using Tweedy Plum, CO 32 sts.
Work 8 rows garter st.
Change to St st and work until piece measures 11 in (28 cm).
Work 8 rows garter st. Bind off.

HANDLES
Make 2
Using Tweedy Plum, CO 10 sts.
Work in garter st for 13 in (33 cm).
Bind off.

Rabbit

Make 2
Using cream, CO 12 sts.
Work 2 rows in St st.
Inc 1 st at each end of next and foll alt row until there are 18 sts.
Work 10 rows straight.
Dec 1 st at each end of next and foll alt rows until 12 sts remain.
Work 2 rows St st. Bind off.

Nose
Using cream, CO 6 sts.
Work 2 rows St st.
Inc 1 st at each of next and foll alt rows until there are 12 sts, ending with a purl row.
Work 4 rows St st.
Dec 1 st at each of next and foll alt rows until there are 6 sts.
Work 2 rows and bind off.

Ears
Make 2
Using cream, CO 6 sts.
Work 2 rows in garter st.
Inc 1 st at each end of next and foll alt row (10 sts).
Work 22 rows straight.
K2tog at each end of every row until 4 sts remain. Bind off.

Front feet
Make 2
Using cream, CO 8 sts.
Work in garter st for 10 rows.
Dec 1 st at each of next and foll alt row.

Work 1 row. Bind off.

Back feet
Make 2
Using cream, CO 8 sts.
Work in garter st for 8 rows.
Dec 1 st at each of next row.
Work 6 rows garter st.
K2og at each end of the next 2 rows. Bind off.

Assembling the bag

Fold the bag in half and mark the center line; this denotes back and front surfaces.

Working on the front, place a body on the bag and stitch in place. Sew the muzzle in the center of the body. Before closing the stitching, add a little stuffing to pad lightly. Pleat the top of each ear to give shape, then sew in place at the top center of each side of the body. Sew the front feet onto the base of the body. Embroider the eyes and nose using contrast yarn threaded through a tapestry needle then make a few straight sts on each foot to describe the claws. Sew the butterfly to the top center of the bunny's head.

Sew the other body piece on the bag back, aligning it with the position of the front body. Sew the back feet in place on each side and embroider claws as before. Make a small pompom for the tail. Sew in place. Turn right sides inside and sew the side seams. Turn right side out. Fold each handle in half lengthways and sew the long seam. Sew in place on each side of the bag.

Oswald the Owl

Create your own fun patchwork owl for little ones. Worked in stockinette and garter stitches, he is quite simple to knit. You will need to use separate balls of yarn for some sections and twist them together on the wrong sides of the work when changing colors to avoid holes. His eyes are felt pieces sewn onto a knitted mask. If you don't like the idea of knitting with two balls of yarn at the same time then make the owl in just one color on each piece; he will look just as cute.

✱✱ Intermediate

You will need
1 x 2 oz (50 g) ball of DK yarn in bright pink, turquoise, green and yellow
Oddment of cream 4-ply yarn, for the mask
Scraps of felt in pale blue, black and white, for the eyes
US 5 (UK 9, 3.75 mm) knitting needles
US 3 (UK 10, 3.25 mm) knitting needles
US F 5 (UK 9, 3.75 mm) crochet hook
Polyester fiberfill
Tapestry needle, for sewing up
Sewing kit
Glue

Gauge
Is not critical on this project.

Size
Owl stands 10 in (25 cm) tall

Owl
FRONT RIGHT SIDE
Begin at the base of the owl and using US 5 (UK 9, 3.75 mm) knitting needles and pink yarn, CO 14 sts.
Work 2 rows garter st.
Change to St st and, working in stripes of 2 rows turquoise and 2 rows pink, AT THE SAME TIME increase

1 st at the end of the next row (this is the side edge) and at the same edge on foll alt rows until there are 28 sts on the needle, ending on a purl row.
Break off turquoise and join in green.
Work 12 rows in stripes of 2 rows green, 2 rows pink.
Break off pink.
Cont in green only for 10 rows.
Dec 1 st at the side edge of next and foll 3 alt rows. Purl 1 row. Bind off.

Front left side

Using US 5 (UK 9, 3.75 mm) knitting needles and pink yarn, CO 7 sts, join in yellow and CO 7 sts.
Work 2 rows garter st, keep colors as set and twist yarns tog at center on the wrong side of the work to avoid holes.
Change to St st and inc 1 st at beg of next (this is the side edge) and every foll alt row until there are 28 sts, ending on a purl row.
Change to blue yarn and work in St st for another 22 rows.
Dec 1 st at side edge of next and foll 3 alt rows. Purl 1 row and bind off.

Back left side

Using US 5 (UK 9, 3.75 mm) knitting needles and green yarn, CO 14 sts.
Work 2 rows garter st. Join in yellow yarn and change to St st, working in a stripe sequence of 2 rows yellow and 2 rows green, and AT THE SAME TIME inc 1 st at beg of next (this is the side edge) and every following alt row until there are 28 sts, ending with a purl row.
Work another 12 rows in stripe sequence. Join in turquoise yarn. (Twist yarns together when changing colors to eliminate holes in the work.)
Next row: K14 yellow, K14 turquoise.

Cont in St st for another 9 rows.
Dec 1 st at side edge of next and foll 3 alt rows. Purl 1 row and bind off.

Back right side

Using US 5 (UK 9, 3.75 mm) knitting needles and green yarn, CO 14 sts.
Work 2 rows garter st.
Change to St st and inc 1 st at the end of next (this is the side edge) and foll alt rows until there are 28 sts on the needle.
Work 2 more rows straight. Now join in pink and yellow yarns.
Next row: K14 pink, K14 yellow.
Next row: P14 yellow, P14 pink.
Cont as set for another 12 rows. Break off yellow and pink.
Join in green and work across all stitches for another 6 rows St st.
Dec 1 st at side edge of next row and 3 foll alt rows. Purl 1 row. Bind off.

Feet

Make 4 in garter st
Using US 5 (UK 9, 3.75 mm) knitting needles and turquoise, CO 20 sts.
Knit 4 rows.
Dec 1 st at each end of next and foll alt rows until 4 sts remain.
Knit 2 rows. Bind off.

Wings

Make 4
Using US 5 (UK 9, 3.75 mm) knitting needles and pink, CO 22 sts and work as for feet.

EYE MASK

Using US 3 (UK 10, 3.25 mm) knitting needles and cream 4-ply yarn, CO 10 sts.

Work in garter st throughout.

***Knit 2 rows.

Inc 1 st at each end of next and foll alt rows until there are 22 sts on the needle.

Work 8 rows straight on these stitches.

Dec 1 st at each end of next and foll alt rows until there are 10 sts.***

Work 4 rows garter st on these stitches.

Work from *** to ***. Bind off.

BEAK

Using US 5 (UK 9, 3.75 mm) knitting needles and yellow, CO 3 sts.

Work 1 row garter st.

Row 2: Inc in first and last st.

Row 3: Knit.

Rep last 2 rows once more (7 sts).

Knit 2 rows straight.

Dec 1 st at each end of every alt row until 3 sts remain. K3tog. Finish off.

EAR TUFTS

Make 2 in each of the four colors

Using US F 5 (UK 9, 3.75 mm) crochet hook, ch 25, finish off.

Assembling the owl

Work in all ends on all pieces. With right sides facing, sew the fronts together at the center seam with the shaped sides on the outside. Do the same for the back pieces. Now place back and front together, right sides inside, and sew up base and side seams. Stuff from the top, not too firmly, shaping the owl as you work. Sew the top seam together neatly.

Fold the wings in half and stitch the side seams. Stuff lightly and sew the base. Run a thread through from the base to the center of the wing, pull up and secure to give shape. Sew wings onto each side of the owl. Make the feet in the same way, but run threads through at thirds to shape the toes. Sew to the base of the owl.

Pin the eye mask in place on the center front of the owl; stretch a little when sewing in place to make the mask rounded. For the eyes, cut circles of felt in blue and black. Cut a small V shape out of the black circle on one side. Place the black circle onto the blue circle, then place the eyes on the mask. Glue and sew firmly in place. Cut a tiny circle of white felt and add to each eye; sew in place. Sew the beak between the eyes at the base of the eye mask; stuff lightly.

Fold the ear tufts in half and secure. Taking one of each color, sew in bunches on each side of the owl at the top of his head.

Octavia Octopus

Plain and eyelash yarns are used to create different textures in this friendly octopus.

I have chosen a mix of pale pink and purple, though the toy would be equally as

pretty in stripes or bright colors; you could even make each tentacle in a different

color – a perfect way to use up your stash.

❋❋ Intermediate

You will need

2 x 2 oz (50 g) balls Sirdar Snuggly Pearls DK
   Pearly Lilac, shade 430
2 x 2 oz (50 g) balls Sirdar Funky Fur Eyelash DK
   Angel Pink, shade 533
Small amount of Sirdar Snuggly DK Spicy Pink,
   shade 350
Oddments of black yarn, for the features
US 6 (UK 8, 4 mm) knitting needles
Polyester fiberfill
Tapestry needle, for sewing up
Sewing kit

Gauge

Is not critical on this project.

Size

9 in (23 cm) from base to top of head.

Octopus

BODY
Using Pearly Lilac, CO 84 sts.
Work 2 rows in garter st.
Change to St st and work 34 rows ending on a purl row.
Shape top
Row 1: K3, *K2tog, K4*, rep from * to * ending last rep, K2tog, K1.
Row 2: Purl.
Row 3: K2, *K2tog, K3*, rep from * to * ending last rep, K2tog, K1.
Row 4: Purl.
Row 5: K1, *K2tog, K2*, rep from * to * ending last rep,

Inc 1 st at each end of next and every foll alt row until there are 24 sts.
Work 14 rows straight in garter st.
Dec 1 st at each end of next and foll alt rows until there are 14 sts.
Work 2 rows. Bind off.

Upper tentacles
Make 8
Using Pearly Lilac, CO 10 sts.
Row 1: K4, P2, K4.
Row 2: Knit.
The 2 rows form the pattern.
Work as set for another 44 rows.
Dec at each end of every following row until 4 sts remain by knitting 2 sts tog. Bind off.

Underside of the tentacles
Make 8
Using Angel Pink, CO 10 sts.
Work 46 rows in garter st.
Dec at each end of every row until 4 sts remain, by knitting 2 sts tog. Bind off.

Frill
Using Spicy Pink, CO 160 sts.
Work 6 rows in garter stitch.
Work 8 rows in St st beg with a knit row.
Next row: K2tog all across row.
Bind off purlwise. Finish off.

Bow
(Worked in garter st. Carry yarn not in use up side of work.)
Using Spicy Pink, CO 14 sts.
Work 6 rows Spicy Pink and 4 rows in Angel Pink,

K2tog, K1.
Row 6: Purl.
Row 7: *K2tog, K1*, rep from * to * across row.
Row 8: Purl.
Row 9: K2tog across row.
Break yarn and run through remaining sts on needle, draw up tightly and finish off.

Base of body
Using Angel Pink, CO 14 sts.
Working in garter st throughout, knit 2 rows.

alternating the colorways as you go.
Rep the last 10 rows twice more.
Work 12 rows Spicy Pink.
**Work 4 rows Angel Pink, then 6 rows Spicy Pink.
Repeat last 10 rows twice more.
Work 4 rows Angel Pink and 12 rows Spicy Pink.**
Work from ** to ** once more.
Work 4 rows Angel Pink, 6 rows Spicy Pink.
Rep last 10 rows three times more. Bind off.
Work in any loose ends on the strip of knitting. Join
the two short ends together. The join will be in the
center of the underside. Thread a needle with pink yarn
and sew the bow together in the center through both
thicknesses. Gather up tightly as you work to form the
bow shape.

Assembling the octopus

Sew the side seam of the body (the seam runs down
the center back). Stuff quite firmly to give a nice
round shape. Pin the base in place all around the body,
stretching it to fit quite tightly. Add extra stuffing, if
needed, before sewing closed. Manipulate into shape,
flattening the base of the body as you do. Sew the
tentacles together in pairs, one lilac and one pink,
matching one short straight end and with the eyelash
yarn on the underside. Note that the undersides of the
tentacles are slightly longer than the upper tentacles.
Curl up the ends of the tentacles, making each one of
them vary in length, and sewing in place as you go. Pin
the tentacles evenly around the base of the body. Sew
firmly in place.

Join the short ends of the skirt together. Run some
Spicy Pink all around the bind-off edge. Slip the skirt
onto the octopus and gather up slightly to fit tightly
around the body. Stitch in place. Embroider the facial
details. Sew the bow to one side of the head.

Duckling Crib Toy

Knit this sweet little toy to keep a tiny baby amused while in a crib or stroller. Pretty bows decorated with attractive flower buttons alternate with cute ducklings. Loops at each end can be used to string the toy across the crib.

✳✳ Intermediate

You will need

1 x 2 oz (50 g) ball ball Sirdar Snuggly DK Lemon, shade 252
Small amounts of DK yarn in turquoise, pale blue, pale green and orange
Black DK yarn, for the eyes
4 flower buttons
US 5 (UK 9, 3.75 mm) knitting needles
US D 3 (UK 10, 3.25 mm) crochet hook
Polyester fiberfill

Gauge

Is not critical on this project.

Ducklings

Make 3
Begin at base: Using Lemon, CO 8 sts.
Row 1: Purl.
Row 2: Inc in every st (16 sts).
Row 3: Purl.
Row 4: *K1, inc*, rep from * to * to end (24 sts).
Row 5: Purl.
Row 6: *K2, inc*, rep from * to * to end (32 sts).
Row 7: Purl.
Work 20 rows St st.
Row 28: *K2, k2tog*, rep from * to * across row.
Row 29: Purl.
Row 30: *K1, K2tog*, rep from * to * across the row.
Row 31: Purl.
Row 32: K2tog across row.
Row 33: Purl.

Break yarn and thread through sts on needles. Draw up tight and finish off.

FEET
Make 1
Using orange, CO 4 sts.
Knit 1 row.
Row 2: Inc in first and last st.
Row 3: Knit.
Repeat last 2 rows until there are 10 sts.
Knit 4 rows. Bind off.

BEAK
Using US 5 (UK 9, 3.75 mm) knitting needles and orange, CO 1 st.
Row 1: Inc in st.
Row 2: Inc in first st, K1.
Row 3: Knit.
Row 4: Inc in first and last st (6 sts).
Row 5: K2tog at each end of row.
Row 6: Knit.
Row 7: K2tog at each end of row.
Row 8: K2tog and finish off.

HANGING LOOPS
Make 2
Using US D 3 (UK 10, 3.25 mm) hook and Lemon, ch 12, join into a circle with a sl st.
Work 34 sc into ring, join as before, and finish off.
Sew the seam on the body piece, noting that the seam runs down the back of the duck. Leave a gap about half way down, stuff firmly, then close up the gap. Mark 8 rows down from the start of the head shaping. Take a needle threaded with yarn and run the yarn all around the marked row, starting and ending at the back seam. Draw up firmly to make the head, rearranging the

stuffing, if necessary. Secure the thread. Using black yarn, embroider the eyes. Take the beak and fold it in half. Sew the center fold to the head. Sew a line through the center of the feet and gather slightly to give shape. Sew to the base of the duckling.

BOWS
Make 4
Using your choice of color, CO 8 sts.
Work in garter st for 60 rows. Bind off.
Stitch the short ends together. Flatten the loop so that the join is at the center back. Take a needle and matching yarn, and make a running st through the center, from top to bottom. Gather up the stitches to create a bow. Secure with a few stitches. Sew a flower button to the center of each bow.

Assembling the toy
Sew the bows and ducklings tog, beg with a bow and alternating the shapes. Sew a hanging loop to each end.

Petals Baby Grab Toy

This adorable baby grab toy is made using different stitches, bobbles, and cables to create textures for Baby's little hands to explore. On one side the little flower is fast asleep, and on the other she is wide awake and ready to play. Add a hanging loop and use the flower as a crib toy, if you like.

✳✳ Intermediate

You will need
Oddments of bright colors in DK weight yarn
US 3 (UK 10, 3.25 mm) knitting needles
Cable needle
Polyester fiberfill
Tapestry needle, for sewing up
Sewing kit

Size
8¼ in (21 cm)

Special abbreviations
MB = make bobble: Knit 3 times into next stitch by knitting first into the front and then into the back and then into the front again. Turn, P4. Turn, K4. Turn, P4. Turn, K4.

Lift second, third and fourth stitches over the first stitch, one at a time to create a bobble.
C4B = cable 4 sts to the back: slip next 2 sts onto a cable needle and leave at the back of the work, knit the next 2 sts, then knit the 2 sts from the cable needle.

Flower
FLOWER CENTER
Make 2
Using choice of color, CO 10 sts.
Knit 2 rows garter st.
Inc 1 st at each end of next and foll alt rows until there are 24 sts.
Work 18 rows straight on these stitches continuing in garter st.
Dec 1 st at each end of next and foll alt rows until

10 sts remain.
Knit 2 rows. Bind off.

Petal 1
Make 6
Using color of your choice, CO 8 sts.
Knit 2 rows garter st.
Inc 1 st at each end of next and foll alt rows until there are 14 sts.
Work straight for 8 rows in garter st.
Dec 1 st at end of next and foll alt rows until there are 2 sts, K2tog. Finish off.

Petal 2
Make 6
Using color of choice, CO 9 sts.
Work in seed st as follows:
Row 1: *K1, P1*, rep from * to * across row, to last st, K1.
Row 2: As Row 1.
Working the inc stitches into the pattern, inc 1 st at each of next and foll alt rows until there are 15 sts.
Work 8 rows seed st.
Dec 1 st at each end of next and foll alt rows until 3 sts remain, K3tog. Finish off.

Petal 3
Make 6
Follow instructions for Petal 1 but work in stripes of 2 rows main color, 2 rows contrast.

Cable ring
Using color of your choice, CO 14 sts.
Row 1: P2, K4, P2, K4, P2.
Row 2: K2, P4, K2, P4, K2.
Row 3 P2, C4B P2, C4B, P2.

Row 4: As Row 2.
Row 5: As Row 1.
Row 6: As Row 2.
Rep these 6 rows until work is long enough to fit around the inner circle of the face, ending on a row 6. Bind off.

Bobble ring
Using color of your choice, CO 7 sts.
Knit 4 rows in garter st.
Next row: K3, MB, K3.
Work 5 rows garter st.
Rep last 6 rows until work fits around the inner circle of the face ending on a garter st row. Bind off.

Assembling the flower
Sew the two flower centers together around the edge leaving a small opening to stuff the shape. Stuff lightly and sew the gap closed. Stitch the petals together in pairs around the sides and leave the base open. Stuff each lightly then sew the opening closed. Arrange the petals around the flower center, pin in position, then stitch firmly in place. Embroider a smiley face on one side of the center and a sleepy face on the other side. Fold the cable strip in half lengthways, stitch the seam, then join the strip into a circle. Repeat with the bobble strip. Sew a cable circle to the outer edge of one flower center and a bobble circle to the other flower center to cover the joins of the petals.

Pete the Penguin

Make this cheerful little fellow to bring a smile to someone's face. With his chubby tummy and cheeky face he is sure to become a firm favorite with all ages.

✳ Beginner

You will need
3 x 1 oz (25 g) balls Robin DK White, shade 70
3 x 1 oz (25 g) balls Robin DK Raven (black), shade 89
2 x 1 oz (25 g) balls Robin DK Gold, shade 286
Polyester fiberfill
US 6 (UK 8, 4 mm) knitting needles

Gauge
Is not critical for this project.

Size
From base to top of head 12 in (30 cm)

Penguin
Body and head are knitted in one piece.

BACK
Using Raven, CO 20 sts.
Work 4 rows St st.
Row 5: *K1, inc in next st* rep from * to * to end (30 sts).
Work 9 rows St st.
Row 15: *K2, inc in next st*, rep from * to * to last st, K1 (40 sts).
Work 27 rows in St st.
Row 43: *K2, K2tog*, across row to last st, K1 (40 sts).
Row 44: Purl. (When knitting Front only change to Raven here.)
Work 2 rows St st.
Row 47: K2tog at each end of row (28 sts).

Row 48: Purl.
Work 2 rows St st.
Row 51: K2tog at each end of row (26 sts).
Row 52: Purl.
Row 53: *K2, K2tog*, rep from * to * to last
2 sts, K2 (20 sts).
Work 5 rows St st.
Row 59: *K2, K2tog*, rep from * to * to end (15 sts).
Row 60: Purl.
Row 61: *K2tog,* rep from * to * to last st K1 (8 sts).
Break yarn and thread through sts on needles. Draw up
and finish off.

Front
Work as for back, but use White to begin with and then
change to Raven as stated in the instructions.

Wings
Make 2
Using Raven, CO 5 sts.
Row 1: Knit.
Row 2: K2, M1, K1, M1, K2 (7 sts).
Row 3: Knit.
Row 4: K3, M1, K1, M1, K3 (9 sts).
Row 5: Knit.
Cont to inc in this way on every other row, adding the
extra stitches on each side as set until there are 15 sts.
Work 6 rows in garter st.
Next row: K2tog at each end of row.
Next row: Knit.
Rep last 2 rows until 3 sts remain.
K3tog and finish off.

Mask
Using White, CO 28 sts.
Work 8 rows St st.
Row 9: K2tog at each end of row.
Row 10: Purl.
Row 11: K2tog, K9, K2tog, turn and work first side.
Row 12: Purl.
Row 13: K2tog, K7, K2tog.
Row 14: Purl.
Row 15: K2tog, K5, K2tog.
Row 16: Purl. Bind off.
Return to rem sts and complete to match first side.

Feet
Make 2
Using Gold, CO 20 sts.

Knit 4 rows.
Dec 1 st at each end of next and every foll alt row until
4 sts remain.
Knit 4 rows.
Inc 1 st at each end of next and foll alt rows until there
are 20 sts.
Knit 4 rows. Bind off.

BEAK
Using Gold, CO 8 sts.
Knit 2 rows.
Dec 1 st at each end of next and foll alt rows until 2
sts remain. K2tog. Finish off.

Assembling the penguin

Sew the back and front body together, leaving the
base open for stuffing. Stuff firmly and mold into a
rounded ball. Pin the mask in position on the front of
the penguin. Sew in place, stretching a little to get the
rounded shape and ensuring each side is even. Sew the
beak in the center of the mask. Embroider the eyes on
each side of the beak.
Sew the wings to each side of the penguin. Fold the
feet in half.
Sew the side seams, add some stuffing to give shape,
and sew the base. Take some matching yarn and sew
through from the base to the front of the foot in three
places, radiating out from a single point at the base.
Pull each point slightly to cause an indentation and
create toes on the feet. Sew feet to base, angling them
outward slightly.

Sweetheart Blanket

Keep Baby "snug as a bug in a rug" with this cute patchwork cover. I have designed it using garter stitch squares, with the addition of a relief-work heart made up of knit and purl stitches. I have chosen traditional mixtures of pinks but you can mix and match whatever colors you like best. An easy crochet edging completes the cover. If you can't crochet then just leave the blanket edge plain; it will look just as pretty.

✳✳ Intermediate

You will need
1 x 3½ oz (100 g) ball Aran-weight baby yarn
  in each of four matching shades (A, B, C, D)
US 8 (UK 6, 5 mm) knitting needles
US F 5 (UK 9, 3.75 mm) crochet hook
Tapestry needle, for sewing up
Sewing kit

Gauge
Each square measures 6 in (15 cm).

Size
24 in (60 cm) square

Blanket
The blanket is made in four strips, each containing 4 squares. Each strip is worked in a specific color and pattern sequence.
Working from right to left, strips appear as follows:
Strip 1: D with heart, A plain, C with heart, B plain.
Strip 2: C plain, B with heart, D plain, A with heart.
Strip 3: B with heart, C plain, A with heart, D plain.
Strip 4: A plain, D with heart, B plain, C with heart.

Plain square

Make 2 plain squares in each of the 4 colors: 8 in total
CO 25 sts.
Work 44 rows in garter st. Bind off.

Heart square

Make 2 heart squares in each of the 4 colors: 8 in total
CO 25 sts.
Work 10 rows garter st.
Begin heart pattern:
Row 11: Knit.
Row 12: K12, P1, K12.
Row 13: Knit.
Row 14: K10, P5, K10.
Row 15: Knit.
Row 16: K8, P9, K8.
Row 17: Knit.
Row 18: K6, P13, K6.
Row 19: Knit.
Row 20: K5, P15, K5.
Row 21: Knit.
Row 22: As Row 20.
Row 23: Knit.
Row 24: As Row 20.
Row 25: Knit.
Row 26: As Row 20.
Row 27: Knit.
Row 28. K5, P7, K1, P7, K5.
Row 29: Knit.
Row 30: K6, P5, K3, P5, K6.
Row 31: Knit.
Row 32: K7, P3, K5, P3 K7.
Row 33: Knit.
Row 34: K8, P1, K7, P1, K8.
Rows 35–44: Knit.
Bind off.

Assembling the blanket

Work in ends neatly. Sew strips together with right
sides facing, joining the garter st row by row with a
matching yarn and blunt-ended sewing needle. Take
the needle through alternate rows of adjacent squares,
picking up the "little bump" made by the garter st.
Draw together firmly to give an almost invisible seam.

Edging

Starting at one corner of the rug, join Yarn C and work
a row of sc all around the edge, working between each
garter st ridge on the side of the squares and each
stitch along the cast-on and bind-off edges. Work 3 sc
into each corner to keep the edge flat.
Do not turn work but join in yarn B, and work 1 sc into
each sc around rug and AT THE SAME TIME work 3 sc
into each corner sc. Work 2 more rounds in A. Join D
and work 1 round in sc.
Turn, work into each sc as follows for last row: *1 dc,
1 sl st*, rep from * to * all around rug. Join with a sl st.
Do not increase in the corners on this round. Finish off
and work in ends.

Henry the Hedgehog

With his bright red striped scarf and beady eyes, Henry is all set for an afternoon adventure out. His prickles have been replaced with a loop stitch pattern that makes him very cuddly. He's quite simple to knit, though the loop stitch part of his back takes a little time and patience to create.

❄❄ Intermediate

You will need

1 x 2 oz (50 g) ball of Sirdar Snuggly Snowflake DK Beige, shade 642 (A)
1 x 2 oz (50 g) ball of Bergere de France Cosmos Marron/Ecru shade 29084 (B)
Oddments of DK in red, white, and black
2 x ¼ in (6 mm) black safety eyes
US 7 (UK 7, 4.5 mm) knitting needles
US 5 (UK 9, 3.75 mm) knitting needles
Polyester fiberfill
Tapestry needle, for sewing up
Sewing kit

Special abbreviations

LS = Loop stitch. Insert the needle as for plain and knit 1 st, keeping it on the right-hand needle, but do not slip the stitch off the left-hand needle; pass the wool to the front (as for purl) and hold under thumb, then back between the needles; knit into the same stitch and slip off; pass the first stitch over the second.

Hedgehog

Body

Make 2

Using US 7 (UK 7, 4.5 mm) knitting needles and Yarn A, CO 10 sts.

Work 2 rows St st.

Row 3: Inc 1 st each end of row.

Work 3 rows St st.

Rep last 4 rows until there are 22 sts.

Work 4 rows straight in St st.

Dec 1 st at each end of next and every foll third row

until 12 sts remain.
Bind off. (This is the neck edge).

HEAD

Using US 7 (UK 7, 4.5 mm) knitting needles and Yarn A, CO 12 sts.
Work 2 rows St st.
Row 3: Knit, increasing in every stitch to end of row (24 sts).
Row 4: Purl.
Row 5: K1, *inc in next st, K1*, rep from * to * to end of row (36 sts).
Beg with a purl row, work 3 rows St st.
Row 9: K1, *inc in next st, K2*, rep from * to * to last 2 sts, inc in next st, K1.
Beg with a purl row, work 7 rows in St st.
Shape face and nose:
Row 17: *K2, K2tog, K2*, rep from * to * to end of row (40 sts).
Beg with a purl row, work 3 rows St st.
Row 21: *K2, K2tog, K1*, rep from * to * to end of row (32 sts).
Beg with a purl row, work 3 rows St st.
Row 25: *K1, K2tog, K1*, rep from * to * to end of row (24 sts).
Row 26: Purl.
Row 27: *K1, K2tog* to end of row (16 sts).
Row 28: Purl.
Row 29: K2tog all across row (8 sts). Break off Yarn A. Change to black DK and work 6 rows St st. Run yarn through the 8 sts and draw up tightly. Finish off.

PRICKLES

Work 2-row pattern as follows:
Row 1: K1, loop st (LS) to last st, K1.
Row 2: Purl.

Using US 7 (UK 7, 4.5 mm) knitting needles and Yarn B, CO 3 sts. (This end of work will be stitched centrally onto the head just above the eyes; refer to photograph for guidance.)
Knit 2 rows St st.
Row 3: Inc in first st, LS 1, inc in last st.
Row 4: Purl.
Row 5: Inc in first st, LS 3, inc in last st.
Row 6: Purl.
Row 7: Inc in first st, LS 5 , inc in last st.
Row 8: Purl (9 sts).
Row 9: CO 3 sts, LS to last st, K1.
Row 10: CO 3 sts, purl to end.
Row 11: CO 4 sts, LS to last st, K1.
Row 12: CO 4 sts, purl to end.
Row 13: CO 4 sts, LS to last st, K1.
Row 14: CO 4 sts, purl to end (27 sts).
Keeping the loop st patt correct, inc 1 st at each end on next and foll alt rows until there are 33 sts, ending on a purl row. Cont on these 33 sts working in loop pattern until there are 21 rows of loops, ending on a row 2.
Dec 1 st at each end of the next and foll alt row (29 sts).
Next row: Purl.
Keeping patt correct, bind off 4 sts at the beg of next 4 rows.
Bind off remaining 13 sts.

Ears

Make 2

Using US 7 (UK 7, 4.5 mm) knitting needles and Yarn
A, CO 6 sts.

Knit 4 rows.

Row 5: K2tog at each end of next row.

Row 6: K2tog at each end of next row.

Row 7: K2tog, finish off.

Feet

Make 4

Using US 7 (UK 7, 4.5 mm) knitting needles and Yarn A,
CO 20 sts.

Work 10 rows St st.

Dec 1 st at each end of every alt row until
10 sts remain, end with a purl row.

Next row: K2tog all across row (5 sts).

Next row: P5tog. Finish off.

Scarf

Carry yarn not in use neatly up the side of the work.
Do not pull too tightly or work will pucker.

Using US 5 (UK 9, 3.75 mm) knitting needles and
white DK, CO 8 sts.

Work in garter st stripes of 6 rows white and 6 rows
red. Cont until work has 14 red stripes, ending with a
white stripe. Bind off.

Assembling the hedgehog

Sew in all ends neatly on all pieces. Note that the
reverse St st is the right side of the work on the body,
head and feet.

Turn head piece right sides inside. Sew the head seam
together from the nose end, leaving an opening to
stuff the piece. Turn right side out. Insert the safety
eyes and ensure they are firmly fixed. Stuff the head to
give a round shape, and make sure the nose is firm and
round. Close the opening and finish off. Stitch a smiley
mouth using black yarn.

With right sides inside, stitch body pieces together,
leaving neck edge open for stuffing. Turn right sides
out and stuff body, giving it a rounded shape. Close
opening and secure. Stitch head onto the body, making
sure it's centrally positioned and very secure.

With right sides inside, sew feet together, leaving base
open for stuffing. Turn right sides out, stuff to give
a rounded shape, stitch up base and secure. Using
matching cotton thread and a sharp needle, form the
toes. Insert the thread at the center of a foot, pull
over to opposite side of foot, thread through to the
side where you began and pull firmly; this will make
indentations into the piece to denote the shape of the
toes. Repeat twice more, then secure the cotton firmly.
Stitch the feet in position.

Work in all scarf ends. Tie the scarf around the neck,
and secure with a few stitches.

Work in all ends of prickles piece neatly. Stitch the
pointed end of the prickles onto the head just above
the eyes. Position the rest of this section around the
back of the head and body, stuffing lightly as you go
to give shape to the prickles. When you are happy with
the look, stitch in place around the head and body of
the hedgehog. Stitch the ears in place, one on each
side of the head.

Sydney Snake

This toy can be made using oddments of yarn from your stash, I have suggested a color scheme but you can use whatever bright shades you have to hand and change the sequence to suit your own shades.

✳✳ Intermediate

You will need
Oddments of Sirdar Snuggly DK in 7 bright colors,
   1 oz (25 g) (1 ball) each of pink, mint, mid green,
   red, yellow, turquoise, denim blue
Oddment of black yarn, for the eyes
US 6 (UK 8, 4 mm) knitting needles
Polyester fiberfill
Tapestry needle, for sewing up
Sewing kit

Size
Snake measures 27 in (69 cm) from head to tip of tail

Snake
Begin at head

Stripe sequence: Pink, mint, mid green, red, yellow, turquoise.

Using US 6 (UK 8, 4 mm) needles and yellow, CO 16 sts.
Row 1: Purl.
Row 2: Increase knitwise into every stitch (32 sts).
Row 3: Purl.
Row 4: *K2, inc in next st*, rep from * to * to last 2 sts, K2 (42 sts).
Beg with a purl row, work 21 rows St st.
Row 26: Purl, decreasing 6 sts evenly across the row (36 sts).

Begin body pattern:

Rows 1–2: St st in denim blue knit.

Row 3: Join in pink yarn, K1, sl 2, *K6, sl 2*, rep from * to * to last st, K1.

Row 4: Using pink, P1, sl 2, *P6, sl 2*, rep from * to * last st, P1.

Rep the last 2 rows twice more.

Rows 9–10: Knit, using denim blue.

Row 11: Join in mint, K5, sl 2, *K6, sl 2*; rep from * to * to last 5 sts, K5.

Row 12: Using mint, P5, sl 2, *P6, sl 2*, rep from * to * to last 5 sts, P5.

Rep the last 2 rows twice more.

These 16 rows form the pattern.

Cont using denim blue but alternate the colors in the sequence of pink, mint, mid green, yellow, and turquoise until 13 stripes have been worked.

Keeping pattern correct, dec 1 st at each end of row on next and foll 8th rows until there are 28 sts.

Cont working in stripes of 2 rows denim blue garter st and 2 rows turquoise in St st, and AT THE SAME TIME, dec 1 st at each end of the next and foll 4th rows until 20 sts remain.

Cont in denim blue only and St st, and AT THE SAME TIME, dec 1 st at each end of the following fifth rows until there are 10 sts.

Change to red. Continuing in St st, work 18 rows, decreasing at each end as before on each foll 6th row (4 sts).

Next row: K2tog twice.

Next row: K2tog.

Using red, CO 40 sts.

Knit 1 row. Bind off.

Assembling the snake

There are a lot of ends of yarns to work in so use them as best you can to stitch up each stripe on the snake. Starting at the head end, begin to sew the seam (this will run under the body and head of the snake). Stuff the head quite firmly and continue to stuff and shape as you work along the body. Add a small amount of stuffing to the tail. Mold the body of the snake to get a good, even shape.

Fold the tongue in half lengthways. Push the center of the piece inwards to form a letter "Y" and then stitch the piece together to form the tongue. Sew firmly to the center of the mouth. Using black yarn, embroider eyes on the snake, pulling them in quite firmly to give shape to the head.

Rosie the Rag Doll

Every little girl loves a doll to play with and Rosie will be the perfect companion, with her pretty skirt and matching top embroidered with flowers. Her hair is tied in neat braids, and she has matching pink bows.

❋❋ Intermediate

You will need
Wendy Peter Pan DK in the following shades
1 x 2 oz (50 g) ball Wendy Peter Pan DK Powder Pink, shade 927
1 x 2 oz (50 g) ball Wendy Peter Pan DK White, shade 300
1 x 2 oz (50 g) ball Wendy Peter Pan DK Pistachio, shade 922
1 x 2 oz (50 g) ball Wendy Peter Pan DK Rose, shade 381
1 x 2 oz (50 g) ball Wendy Peter Pan DK Milk Chocolate, shade 917
Oddments of black and deep pink 4-ply yarn, for the features
Polyester fiberfill
US 6 (UK 8, 4 mm) knitting needles
Tapestry needle, for sewing up

Sewing kit

Gauge
Is not critical on this project.

Size
13¼ in (36 cm) tall

Doll

The body and head are worked all in one piece.
Using White, CO 36 sts.
Work 16 rows in St st.
Work 4 rows in garter st.
Change to Powder Pink.
Work 24 rows St st, mark this row with a loop of contrast thread for neckline.
Work 26 rows St st.
Next row: K2tog all across row.
Next row: Purl.
Next row: K2tog across row.
Next row: Purl.
Break yarn and run through sts on needle, draw up tightly and finish off.

Arms

Make 2
Using Powder Pink, CO 9 sts for top of the arm.
Purl 1 row.
Row 2: Inc in each st to end of row (18 sts).
Cont in St st for another 20 rows.
Row 23: *K2, inc in next st*, rep from * to * across row (24 sts).
Row 24: Purl.
Work 6 rows St st.
Row 31: K2tog across row (12 sts).
Row 32: Purl.
Row 33: K2tog across row (6 sts).
Break yarn and run thread through sts on needle, draw up and finish off.

Legs

Make 2
Using Powder Pink, CO 20 sts.
Work 28 rows St st.

Break yarn and join in Pistachio for the shoe.
Work 2 rows St st.
Row 3: K13, turn.
Row 4: P6, turn.
Row 5: K6 turn.
Rep last 2 rows twice more.
Break off yarn.
Rejoin yarn to stitches on right-hand needle and proceed as follows:
Pick up and K5 along the side of instep, 6 sts across toe, 5 sts down other side of instep, then knit across sts on left-hand needle.
Next row: Knit across all sts on needle.
Work 4 rows garter st.
Next row: K2tog, K12, K2tog, K12, K2tog.
Next row: K2tog, knit to last 2 sts, K2tog.
Next row: K9, sl 1, K2tog, psso, K9, K2tog.
Bind off.

Shoe straps

Make 2
Using Pistachio, CO 22 sts.
Knit 1 row and bind off.

Hair Bows

Make 2
Using Rose, CO 5 sts.
Work 50 rows in garter st. Bind off.
Sew together the short ends. Fold piece in half with seam on the underside. Now take a needle and matching thread and gather the center of the piece up firmly to make a bow. Secure with stitches.

Top

Make 2
Using Rose, CO 24 sts.

Work 4 rows garter st.
Work 28 rows St st.
Work 4 rows garter st. Bind off.

SLEEVES
Make 2
Using Rose, CO 24 sts.
Work 4 rows garter st.
Work 16 rows St st.
Work 4 rows garter st. Bind off.

SKIRT
Using Pistachio, CO 38 sts.
Work 4 rows garter st.
Work 2 rows St st.
Row 7: *K1, inc,* rep to end (76 sts).
Row 8: Purl.
Change to Rose. Work 4 rows St st.
Row 13: *K3, inc*, rep from * to * to last st, K1
(95 sts).
Row 14: Purl.
Change to Pistachio. Work 6 rows St st.
Change to Rose. Work 4 rows St st.
Now work in garter st for the border:
Work 2 rows Pistachio, 2 rows Rose and 2 rows
Pistachio. Bind off.

Assembling the doll

Sew body and head sections together, leaving base
open to stuff. Seam will run down the back of the doll.
Stuff the head section first, then semi-stuff the body.
Take a needle and matching yarn and beg at the back
seam on the marked neck row, weave the yarn in and
out of every stitch; pull up tight to form the head. Cont
to stuff the body section but do not close the base.
Set aside.

Take the arms and sew the seam, leave the top open to
stuff, then stuff quite firmly, shaping the hand as you
do. Leave enough fabric at the top of the arm to enable
you to sew the arms to the body.
Sew through one side of the hand to form the thumb,
rep on the other hand. Sew the arms to the body
on each side of the shoulders. Embroider the facial
features.
Starting at the foot, sew the sole and back leg seam,
matching colors as you stitch. Leave the top open to
stuff. Stuff the foot section first, then the rest of the
leg. Fold the top of the leg flat with the seam down
the center back. Pin the legs in place inside the base of
the body. Sew the body and legs together at the same
time.
Sew the shoe straps in place around the ankles.
Embroider a flower on the front of each shoe.
To make the hair, wind lengths of yarn around a book
or stiff piece of cardboard approximately 12 in (30 cm)
long. Arrange bunches of yarn across the head, sewing
in place along the center line. Cont to arrange bunches
and sew them in place until the head is covered. Trim
the fringe. Now divide the hair into 11 sections. Plait
(braid) each section fairly loosely. Secure to the head.
Divide the remaining loose ends of the plaits into two
bunches. Tie each bunch tightly. Now sew the Rose
knitted bows securely to each bunch.

Assembling the skirt and top

Sew the back seam on the skirt and slip onto the doll. Secure the skirt to the waist. Sew the shoulder edges of the back and front tog. Fold sleeve in half lengthways, mark center point on bind-off edge. Place this point to center join of back and front at shoulders. Sew sleeves in place onto back and fronts. Fold top in half and sew side and sleeve seams. Embroider flowers onto front of top, if desired. Slip top on to doll. It's easier to put the legs through the neck edge first and pull the top up over the doll's body. Catch the shoulders a little on each side to keep the top in place.

Freddy Fox

This little fellow is waiting for a playmate. He has a cunning smile and big bushy tail to add to his endearing character. Knitted in simple stockinette stitch, he can be attempted by most knitters.

** Intermediate

You will need
1 x 4 oz (100 g) ball Stylecraft Life DK Copper, shade 2312
1 x 4 oz (100 g) ball Stylecraft Life DK Cream, shade 2305
Oddment of black DK for the nose, ears and tail tip
Polyester fiberfill
US 6 (UK 8, 4 mm) knitting needles
Tapestry needle, for sewing up
Sewing kit

Gauge
Is not critical on this project.

Size
12 in (30 cm) when sitting

Fox
HEAD
Using Copper, CO 6 sts.
Row 1: Purl.
Row 2: Inc in each st to end (12 sts).
Row 3: Purl.
Row 4: Inc in each st to end (24 sts).
Row 5: Purl.
Row 6: *K1, inc in next st*, rep from * to * to end (36 sts).
Row 7: Purl.
Work 20 rows St st (mark this final row as the nose line).
Change to Cream and work another 12 rows St st.
Row 40: K2tog across row (18 sts).
Beg with a purl row, work 3 rows St st.
Row 44: K2tog across row (9 sts).
Do not bind off; run yarn through sts on needle, draw

up tightly and secure.

BODY

Using Copper, CO 10 sts.
Work 2 rows St st.
Row 3: Inc in every st (20 sts).
Beg with a purl row, work 3 rows St st.
Row 7: *Inc in next st, K1*, rep from * to * to end (30 sts).
Beg with a purl row, work 5 rows St st.
Row 13: *K2, inc in next st*, rep from * to * to end (40 sts).
Beg with a purl row, work 5 rows St st.
Row 19: *K3, inc in next st*, rep from * to * to end (50 sts).
Beg with a purl row, work 7 rows St st.
Row 27: *K3, K2tog*, rep from * to * to end.
Row 28: Purl.
Work 4 rows St st.
Row 33: *K2, K2tog*, rep from * to * to end.
Row 34: Purl.
Work 8 rows St st.
Row 43: *K1, k2tog*, rep from * to * to end.
Row 44: Purl.
Work 4 rows St st.
Row 49: *K1, K2tog*, rep across row to last 2 sts, K2.
Row 50: Purl.
Row 51: K2tog across row.
Bind off.
Finish off. This is the neck edge.

Arms

Make 2

Using Copper, CO 14 sts.

Work 2 rows St st.

Inc 1 st at each end of next and foll alt rows until there are 24 sts.

Work 13 rows St st.

Next row: *Inc in next st, K2*, rep from * to * across row (32 sts).

Work 9 rows St st.

Next row: *K2tog, K2*, rep from * to * across row (24 sts).

Next row: Purl.

Next row: K2tog all across row (12 sts).

Next row: Purl.

Next row: K2tog across row (6 sts).

Bind off.

Legs

Make 2

Using Copper, CO 14 sts.

Work 2 rows St st.

Inc 1 st at each end of next and foll alt rows until there are 26 sts, ending on a knit row.

Work 15 rows St st.

Next row: K2, *inc in next st, K2*, rep from * to * to end (34 sts). Mark last row with contrast thread as place to gather the paws.

Work 9 rows St st.

Next row: *K2tog, K2*, rep from * to * across row to last st, K1 (236 sts).

Next row: Purl.

Next row: K2tog to end (13 sts).

Next row: Purl.

Next row: K1 *K2tog*, rep from * to * across row (7 sts). Bind off.

Outer Ears

Make 2

Using black, CO 12 sts.

Knit 4 rows St st.

Row 5: K2tog at each end of row.

Row 6: Purl.

Rep last 2 rows until 2 sts remain, K2tog and finish off.

Inner ears

Make 2

Work as for outer ears but use Copper and CO 10 sts instead of 12 sts.

Nose

Using black, CO 8 sts.

Work 4 rows St st.

K2tog at each end of next and foll alt rows until 2 sts remain, K2tog. Finish off.

Bib

Using Cream, CO 10 sts.

Purl 1 row.

Inc 1 st at each end of next and foll alt rows until there are 20 sts ending with a purl row.

Work 6 rows St st straight.

Next row: K2tog at each end of row.

Next row: Purl.

Rep last 2 rows until there are 6 sts rem.

Bind off.

Tail

Using Copper, CO 12 sts.

Work 2 rows St st.

Row 3: Inc in every st (24 sts).

Beg with a purl row, work 5 rows St st.

Row 9: Inc in every st (48 sts).

Beg with a purl row, work 15 rows St st.
Row 25: K3, *K2tog*, rep from * to * to last 3 sts, K3 (39 sts).
Beg with a purl row, work 5 rows St st.
Row 31: *K2, k2tog*, rep from * to * to last 3 sts, K3 (28 sts).
Beg with a purl row, work 5 rows St st.
Break off Copper and join in Cream.
Row 37: *K2, K2tog*, rep from * to * across row.
Beg with a purl row, work 3 rows St st.
Break off Cream and join in black.
Row 41: *K2, K2tog*, rep from * to * to end of row.
Beg with a purl row, work 3 row St st.
Row 45: K2tog across row. Run thread through rem stitches and draw up tight. Finish off.

Assembling the fox

Sew in all ends. Fold the head piece in half and sew the seam, leaving a small opening at one end for stuffing. The seam runs along the underside of the head. Stuff quite firmly and manipulate into shape. Stitch the opening closed. Thread a blunt-ended needle with a length of Cream yarn and run it in and out of every st at the marked row, beg and ending at the seam. Pull the yarn quite firmly to give shape to the nose, secure the yarn with a few holding stitches and work in the ends. Sew the black nose in place and pad out slightly. Embroider the features. Sew pairs of black and Copper ears, pin in position on each side of the head and sew in place. Turn the tops forward slightly.

Fold the body section in half and sew the seam, leaving an opening for stuffing. Stuff firmly and manipulate into shape, then stitch the opening closed. **Note** The seam for the body runs up the center back. Pin the bib in position on the body front and sew in place. Sew the head to the body.

Fold the tail in half and sew the seam. Stuff firmly and manipulate to shape. Attach the tail to the back of the fox. Sew the seams on the arms and legs in the same way, remembering they run on the underside of the pieces. Attach the arms and legs to the body, positioning the legs so that the fox is in a sitting position.

Under-the-Sea Mobile

Cheer up the nursery with this cute and colorful mobile. Baby will love to watch the little fish bobbing around. The fish are simple to knit, though assembling the mobile will take some time and patience.

✳✳ Intermediate

You will need

Oddments of Patons Fairytale Dreamtime DK Lemon, shade 4960

Oddments of Patons Fairytale Dreamtime DK Orange, shade 4951

Oddments of Patons Fairytale Dreamtime DK Lime, shade 4952

Oddments of Patons Fairytale Dreamtime DK Aqua, shade 4957

Oddments of Patons Fairytale Dreamtime DK orange/green multi, shade 4971

Oddments of Patons Fairytale Dreamtime DK blue/aqua multi, shade 4989

Oddments of metallic yarns in matching shades

Black 4-ply floss, for the mouth and eyebrows

16 googly sew-on eyes

8 plastic Christmas balls, each with an 8 in (20 cm) circumference

8 in (20 cm) embroidery hoop

2¼ yd (2.3 m) narrow satin ribbon in each of 4 matching shades

US 3 (UK 10, 3.25 mm) knitting needles

Craft glue

Tapestry needle, for sewing up

Sewing kit

Gauge

Is not critical on this project.

Mobile

FISH BODY

Make 8, mixing and matching the colors

With choice of yarn, CO 4 sts.

Row 1 and following alternate rows: Purl.

Row 2: Inc in each st to end of row (8 sts).

Row 4: Inc in each st to end of row (16 sts).

Row 6: *K1, inc in next st*, rep from * to * to end of row (24 sts).

Row 8: K1, *inc in next st, K2, rep from * to last 2 sts, ending inc, K1 (32 sts).

Row 10: K2, *inc, K3, rep from * to last 2 sts, ending inc, K1 (40 sts).

Work 7 rows St st beg with a purl row.

Row 18: K2, *K2tog, K3*, rep from * to * to last 3 sts, K2tog, K1.

Next and following alt rows: Purl.

Row 20: K1, *K2tog, K2*, rep from * to * to last 3 sts, K2tog, K1.

Row 22: *K1, K2tog*, rep from * to * to end.

Row 24: K2tog across row. Break yarn and run thread through sts on needle, draw up and finish off.

TAIL

Using matching yarn, CO 5 sts.

Work 2 rows garter st and cont in garter st throughout.

Inc 1 st at each end of next and foll alt rows until there are 11 sts.

Work 8 rows straight in garter st.

Dec 1 st at each end of next and foll alt rows until there are 5 sts.

Work 2 rows garter st. Bind off.

FINS

Make 2

Using matching yarn, CO 3 sts.

Work 10 rows St st.

Row 11: K2tog, K1.

Row 12: K2tog and finish off.

Assembling the fish

Slip the body onto a ball and sew in place. Fold the tail in half. Stitch the side seams and leave the base open. Using metallic thread, work lines of chain stitch on each side of the tail. Sew the tail firmly to the back of the fish. Sew a fin on each side of the body. Sew the eyes in place. Using black yarn, embroider a mouth and eyebrows.

Cut ribbon in varying lengths; thread a piece of ribbon through the hanging loop on top of the plastic ball, fold over a small piece at the base and glue firmly in place.

Wind two different colors of ribbon neatly around the embroidery hoop, overlapping them as you work. Glue the ends firmly in place. Glue two equal lengths of ribbon to the top edge of the ring to form the hanging loops.

Attach the ribbons from which the fish dangle evenly around the frame. Wind the ribbon around the frame and glue in place for each of the fish.

Tusker the Elephant

This majestic elephant will delight children of all ages. With his brightly colored blanket and headdress he will cheer up any nursery. He's knitted in seed stitch, which needs to be kept correct throughout his shaping, so for that reason, he's best knitted by those with some experience.

✳✳✳ Experienced

You will need
2 x 4 oz (100 g) balls Cygnet Aran Grey, shade 193

1 x 2 oz (50 g) ball of Patons Diploma Gold DK Royal, shade 6170

1 x 2 oz (50 g) ball of Patons Diploma Gold DK Lemon, shade 6222

1 x 2 oz (50 g) ball of Patons Diploma Gold DK Red, shade 6151

1 x 2 oz (50 g) ball of Patons Diploma Gold DK Apple Green, shade 6125

Small scrap of white DK yarn, for the tusks

Small scrap of silver metallic yarn

Polyester fiberfill

2 black safety eyes

US 7 (UK 7, 4.5 mm) knitting needles

US 6 (UK 8, 4 mm) knitting needles

Stitch holders

Tapestry needle, for sewing up

Sewing kit

Gauge
Using US 7 (UK 7, 4.5 mm) needles, 18 sts measure 4 in (10 cm) wide.

Size
11 in (27 cm) tall

It is very important that you follow the pattern row by row, marking every row as you knit it. There are many increases and decreases worked and they must be made at the correct ends of the pieces. Additionally, the seed stitch pattern has to be kept correct as you work so take care to check that you are following the continuity as you increase or decrease stitches. The elephant is worked entirely in seed stitch unless otherwise stated. Seed stitch is created by alternating 1 knit stitch and 1 purl stitch on every row. The purl stitch is worked over the knitted stitch on the subsequent row. Work a pattern swatch first if you are not familiar with this stitch.

Elephant

Trunk
Make 2

Using US 7 (UK 7, 4.5 mm) needles and Grey, CO 7 sts.
Row 1: (K1, P1) three times, K1.
Row 2: Inc in each of next 2 sts, (K1, P1) twice, K1.
Row 3: Inc in each of next 3 sts, (P1, K1) three times.
Rows 4–5: Keeping seed st correct, inc as for Rows 2–3.
Row 6: Inc in first st, seed st to end.
Row 7: Inc in first st, seed st to end (19 sts).
Work 2 more rows in seed st, break yarn and keep sts on a holder.

Body and head
Make 2

Front leg
****** Using US 7 (UK 7, 4.5 mm) needles and Grey, CO 13 sts.
Work in seed st for 24 rows, leave sts on a spare needle.

Back leg
Work as for front leg for first 19 rows then proceed as follows:
CO 6 sts, seed st to end.
Next row: Seed st to end.
Rep last 2 rows once.
Next row: CO 5 sts, P1, seed st to end.
Next row: Seed st across 30 sts on needle, seed st across 13 sts of Front Leg from spare needle (43 sts).
Mark end of last row with a piece of colored yarn to denote front of elephant.
Seed st 2 rows on these stitches.
Next row: Keeping seed st correct, inc 1 st at each end of row (45 sts).
Work 4 more rows in seed st.******
Next row: Seed st across sts of body, inc in first st of trunk, work across trunk sts, inc in last st (66 sts).
Next row: Work in seed st.
Next row: Work in seed st until 13 sts remain, bind off 5 sts, pattern to end.
Working on the last 8 sts, proceed as follows:
Next row: Work 6 rows in seed st and bind off.
Rejoin yarn to main piece of body.
Row 1: Work in seed st.
Row 2: Seed st to last 2 sts, patt 2tog.
Rows 3–4: Work in seed st.
Row 5: Patt 2tog, seed st to end.
Rows 6–7: As Rows 3–4.
Row 8: As Row 2.
Rows 9–10: As Rows 3–4.
Row 11: Dec 1 st at each end of row.
Rows 12–13: As Rows 3–4.
Row 14: Seed st to last 2 sts, patt 2tog.
Row 15: As Row 14.
Row 16: Work in seed st.
Rows 17–18: Patt 2tog, patt to end.

Rows 19–21: Work in seed st.
Row 22: Dec 1 st at each end of row.
Rows 23–25: As Rows 19–21.
Row 26: Patt 2tog, seed st to end.
Row 27: Dec 1 st at each end of row.
Rows 28–29: As Rows 26–27.
Row 30: Bind off 4 sts, work to last 2 sts, patt 2tog.
Row 31: As Row 26.
Row 32: Bind off 4 sts, seed st to end.
Row 33: Bind off 8 sts, seed st to end.
Row 34: Bind off 6 sts, seed st to end.
Row 35: Bind off remaining sts.

Head gusset

Using US 7 (UK 7, 4.5 mm) knitting needles and Grey,
CO 5 sts (this is the trunk end of the gusset).
Work 26 rows straight in seed st.
Inc 1 st at each end of next and every foll fourth row
until there are 15 sts.
Work 8 rows straight.
Dec 1 st at each end of next row and then every
following fourth row until there are 3 sts, K3tog.
Finish off.

Soles of feet

Make 4 in garter st
Using US 7 (UK 7, 4.5 mm) knitting needles and Grey,
CO 5 sts.
Knit 1 row.
Inc 1 st in every alt row until there are 9 sts.
Knit 4 rows straight.
Dec 1 st at each end of every alt row until there are 5
sts.
Knit 1 row. Bind off.

Under body gusset

Make 2
Work from ****** to ****** on head and body piece.
Work another 2 rows in seed st. Bind off.

Ears

Make 2
Using US 7 (UK 7, 4.5 mm) knitting needles and grey,
CO 5 sts.
Work 1 row seed st.
Inc 1 st at each end of next and foll alt rows until there
are 13 sts.
Work another 9 rows in seed st.
Next row: Inc 1 st at each end of row.
Work 3 rows straight.
Next row: Inc 1 st at beg of row. (Mark beg of this row
to denote outside edge of ear.)
Work 1 row straight.
Next row: Inc 1 st at each end of row.
Next row: Work 1 row straight (18 sts).
Work 5 rows straight in seed st.
Next row: Inc 1 st at beg of row.
Next row: Work 1 row straight.
Dec 1 st at each end of next and foll alt rows.
Bind off 2 sts at the beg of next two rows.
Bind off 3 sts at the beg of next two rows.
Bind off rem sts.

Tail

Take 9 strands of yarn, divide into three equal pieces and make a short plait (braid) about 2¼ in (6 cm) long. Knot the ends and leave a small fringe at the end of each. Attach to back of elephant.

Tusks

Make 2

Using US 6 (UK 8, 4 mm) knitting needles and white, CO 12 sts.

Work 4 rows St st.

Row 5: K2tog at each end of row.

Row 6: Purl.

Rep last 2 rows until 2 sts rem, K2tog, finish off.

Blanket

Carry yarns not in use up the side of work.

Using US 6 (UK 8, 4 mm) needles and Red, CO 34 sts.

Work 2 rows in garter st. Join in silver metallic yarn.

Work 2 rows garter st. Break silver.

Using Red, work 2 more rows garter st.

Join in Lemon and begin patt as follows:

Rows 1–2: Using Lemon, work in St st.

Rows 3–4: Using Royal: K4, *sl 2, K4*, rep from* to * to end.

Rows 5–6: As Rows 1–2.

Rows 7–8: Using Red, K1, sl 2, *K4, sl 2* repeat from * to * to last st, K1.

Rows 9–10: As Rows 1–2.

Rows 11–22: Using Apple Green, work as Rows 3–4.

Rows 13–14: As Rows 1–2.

Rows 15–16: Using Royal, work as Rows 7–8.

Rows 17–18: Work as Rows 1–2.

Rows 19–20: Using Red, work as Rows 3–4.

Rows 21–22: Work as Rows 1–2.

Rows 23–24: Using Apple Green, work as Rows 7–8.

Rep last 24 rows 3 times more, then Rows 1–6 again.

Join in Red and work 2 rows in garter st.

Join in metallic silver and work 2 rows garter st.

Join in Red and work 2 rows garter st. Bind off.

Work in ends.

Edgings

With right side facing and using US 6 (UK 8, 4 mm) needles and Red, pick up and knit 64 sts evenly along one side edge of blanket. Work 1 row garter st in Red. Join in metallic silver and work 2 rows garter st, rejoin Red and work 2 rows garter st. Bind off. Work other edging to match.

Headdress

R = Red and L = Lemon

Note You will need to use separate balls of Red yarn on each side of the Lemon, twisting yarns together when changing colors to avoid holes in your work.

Using US 6 (UK 8, 4 mm) needles and Red, CO 25 sts.

Work 4 rows garter st.

Join in extra balls of yarn.

Row 1: K4 R, K17 L, K4 R.

Row 2: K4 R, K2tog L, K13 Y, K2tog L, K4 R (23 sts).

Row 3: K4 R, K15 L, K4 R.

Row 4: K4 R, K2tog L, K11 L, K2tog L, K4 R (21 sts).

Row 5: K4 R, K13 L, K4 R.

Rows 6–8: Work 3 more rows as set, decreasing as before on next and foll alt row (17 sts).

Row 9: K4 R, P9 L, K4 R.

Row 10: K4 R, K2tog L, K5 L, K2tog L, K4 R (15 sts).

Row 11: K4 R, P7 L, K4 R.

Cont to dec as set until 11 sts remain, ending on a purl row.

Next row: K4 R, K3tog L, K4 R.

Next row: K4 R, P1 L, K4 R.

Next row: K2tog R, K2 R, K1 L, K2 R, K2tog R (7 sts).
Next row: K2tog R, K3 R, K2tog R.
Next row: K5 R.
Next row: Using Red, K2tog, K1, K2tog.
Next row: Using Red, K3tog. Finish off.

Assembling the elephant

Work all ends in on all pieces. With seed st there is no right or wrong side so just reverse the pieces when you sew them up. Join the two underbodies neatly along the bind-off edges.

Join the underbody to main pieces matching legs. Join leg seams. Stitch a sole onto the base of each leg.

Join head gusset to the two main pieces; start at the trunk end and carefully stitch one side at a time onto a main body and head. Run a gathering thread around the end of the trunk, shape and stitch up firmly. Cont to sew up the rest of the head and body. Mark the position of the eyes and either insert safety eyes, or embroider the eyes, if you prefer. Turn the seamed sides inside and stuff the toy. Shape as you stuff. Don't overfill the trunk; it needs to be able to curl a little at the end.

Insert the tail and firmly sew the last part of the body seam.

Work running st around the outside of each ear, pull to gather very slightly to give a rounded shape, and fasten off thread firmly. Place ears on elephant, arranging the shaped edge onto head. Pin in place, ensure they are level and equidistant.

Sew the side seams of the tusks and leave the base open. Stuff firmly. Sew one tusk to each side of the trunk.

Sew in ends on the blanket and headdress. Using a short length of each contrast color, make small tassels and stitch to each corner of the blanket and on the point of the headdress. Sew the headdress onto the elephant's head. Sew the blanket to the elephant's back around the outside edges.

Rainbow Butterfly

This bright and unusual toy with its cute face and rainbow colors is sure to be adored.

It could be used as a crib mobile by attaching a piece of cord firmly to the back and

hanging it up to entertain a little baby.

✳✳ Intermediate

You will need
1 x 2 oz (50 g) ball Patons Fairytale Dreamtime DK
    Orange, shade 4951
1 x 2 oz (50 g) ball Patons Fairytale Dreamtime DK
    Lime, shade 4952
1 x 2 oz (50 g) ball Patons Fairytale Dreamtime DK
    Lemon, shade 4960
1 x 2 oz (50 g) ball Patons Diploma Gold DK Violet,
    shade 6242
1 x 2 oz (50 g) ball Patons Diploma Gold DK Red,
    shade 6151
1 x 2 oz (50 g) ball Patons Fairytale Dreamtime DK
    Aqua, shade 4957
1 x 2 oz (50 g) ball Patons Diploma Gold DK Black,
    shade 6183
US 5 (UK 9, 3.75 mm) knitting needles
US F 5 (UK 9, 3.75 mm) crochet hook

Stitch holder
Polyester fiberfill
Tapestry needle, for sewing up
Sewing kit

Gauge
Is not critical on this project.

Size
9 in (23 cm) long

Butterfly

BODY AND HEAD

Using main color choice, CO 9 sts.

Work in St st for 2 rows.

Cont in St st, inc 1 st at each end of next row.

Row 4: Purl.

Join in contrast color and cont in stripes of 2 rows contrast, 4 rows main, and AT THE SAME TIME inc 1 st at each end of every foll fourth row until there are 21 sts.

Next row: Purl.

Work 14 more rows in stripe pattern.

Keeping continuity of stripe pattern, dec 1 st at each end of next and every foll fourth row until 13 sts remain.

Next row: Purl. Leave this set of sts on a stitch holder or spare needle. Mark this row with a colored thread for the end of the body section.

Now work another piece exactly the same.

Return to set of stitches left on spare needle:

Using contrast color, knit across both sets of 13 sts (26 sts).

Next row: Purl.

Next row: *K2, inc in next st*, rep from * to * to last 2 sts, K2 (34 sts).

Next row: Purl.

Work another 10 rows St st.

Dec as follows:

Next row: *K2, K2tog*, rep from * to * to last 2 sts, K2 (26 sts).

Next row: Purl.

Next row: *K2, K2tog*, rep from * to * to last 2 sts, K2 (20 sts).

Next row: Purl.

Next row: *K2, K2tog*, to end (15 sts).

Next row: Purl.

Next row: K2tog across to last st, K1 (8 sts).

Next row: Purl.

Next row: K2tog all across row (4 sts).

Next row: P4tog. Finish off.

LARGE WINGS

Make 4 wings, 2 in each of 2 colors

Using color of your choice, CO 14 sts.

Work in St st for 4 rows.

Next row: CO 2 sts at beg of row.

Rep last row 3 more times (22 sts).

Inc 1 st at each end of every alt row until there are 28 sts.

Next row: Purl.

Cont in St st for another 12 rows ending on a purl row.

Next row: K1, sl 1, K1, psso, work to last 3 sts, K2tog, K1.

Next row: Purl.

Rep last 2 rows once.

Bind off 3 sts at beg of next 2 rows.

Bind off rem 18 sts.

SMALL WINGS

Make 4 wings, 2 in each of 2 colors

Using color of your choice, CO 12 sts.

Work in St st for 4 rows.

CO 2 sts at beg of every row, 4 times (20 sts).

Inc 1 st at each end of every alt row until there are 24 sts.

Next row: Purl.

Cont in St st for another 10 rows, ending with a purl row.

Next row: K1, sl 1, K1, psso, work to last 3 sts, K2tog, K1.

Next row: Purl.

Repeat the last two rows twice more.

Bind off 3 sts at the beg of next 2 rows.
Bind off rem 14 sts.

LEGS
Make 6
Using crochet hook, crochet a chain in black yarn approximately 5 in (12 cm) long.

FEET
Make 6, each a different color
Using crochet hook and chosen color, ch 3. Now work 10 dc into second chain from hook, join with a sl st to first dc. This will form a little ball; break yarn but leave a long end, thread into a large-eyed needle, then run the yarn all around the top of the ball, threading through the top of each ch. Pull up tightly and secure.

FLOWERS
Using crochet hook and chosen color, ch 6. Join into a ring with a sl st.
Next round: Into ring work (1 sc, 3 ch, 6 times). Join to first sc with a sl st.
Next round: Sl st into first 3 ch space, now work *1 sc, 3 ch, 3 dc, 3 ch, 1 sc* into each space all around. Join with a sl st. Finish off.

ANTENNA
Using crochet hook and black yarn, make a chain approximately 3½ in (8 cm) long. Finish off.

Assembling the butterfly
Work all ends in neatly. With right sides of work facing, join side seams and head seams. Leave the cast-on end sections open to allow for turning and stuffing the piece. Using a small amount of stuffing at a time, firmly stuff the head, then the body. Stitch up the end section neatly. Thread a needle with matching yarn and run it all around the the base of the head section where it joins the body. Weave in and out of the stitches, pull the yarn tightly to form a rounded head, and finish off securely. Do the same on the body section about half way down. This will separate the body into two sections.

Take the antenna and, using a crochet hook, pull the piece through the top of the head from side to side. Make sure the two ends are equal, then secure them onto the head. Roll each end of the antenna into a small circle and secure.

Using black yarn, sew the eyes and a mouth onto the face.

Sew the leg pieces and thread through the upper body section as for the antenna. Space them equally on the center body section, and ensure they are all equal in length, then secure them firmly. Stitch a foot very firmly onto the end of each leg.

Sew a pair of wings with right sides together, leaving the cast-on edges open. Turn right sides out, stuff and shape. Sew the opening closed. Do this on the other pairs of wings. Now stitch together in pairs the 2 large wings and the 2 small wings. Join the two pairs of wings together, and attach firmly to the butterfly's body at the center back. Stitch two crochet flowers in the center back of the wings, and one crochet flower on the top of one of the front wings.

Yarn Information

Bergere de France Cosmos (3% polyester, 11% alpaca, 11% combed wool, 24% cotton, 51% acrylic; 75 m/82 yd)

Bergere de France Plume (11% combed wool, 42% acrylic, 47% polyamide; 60 m/65 yd)

Cygnet Aran (100% acrylic; 210 m/230 yd)

Patons Fairytale Dreamtime DK (100% virgin wool; 90 m/98 yd)

Patons Fairytale Soft DK (55% polyamide, 45% acrylic; 163 m/178 yd)

Patons Diploma Gold DK (55% wool, 25% acrylic, 20% nylon; 120 m/131 yd)

Robin DK (100% acrylic; 300 m/328 yd)

Sirdar Funky Fur Eyelash DK (100% polyester; 90 m/98 yd)

Sirdar Snowflake DK (100% polyester; 85 m/92 yd)

Sirdar Snuggly DK (55% nylon, 45% acrylic; 165 m/179 yd)

Sirdar Snuggly Baby Speckle DK (60% cotton, 40% acrylic; 135 m/148 yd)

Sirdar Snuggly Pearls DK (53% nylon, 43% acrylic, 4% polyester; 170 m/186 yd)

Sirdar Snuggly Tiny Tots DK (90% nylon, 10% polyester; 137 m/150 yd)

Stylecraft Life DK (75% acrylic, 25% wool; 298 m/326 yd)

Wendy Peter Pan DK (55% nylon, 45% acrylic; 170 m/186 yd)

Webs – America's Yarn Store
75 Service Center Road
Northampton, MA 01060
800-367-9327
www.yarn.com
customerservice@yarn.com

Paradise Fibers (Bergere de France yarns)
888-320-7746
www.paradisefibers.com

If you are unable to obtain any of the yarn used in this book, it can be replaced with a yarn of a similar weight and composition. Please note, however, the finished projects may vary slightly from those shown, depending on the yarn used.

For more information on selecting or substituting yarn contact your local yarn shop or an online store, they are familiar with all types of yarns and would be happy to help you. Additionally, the online knitting community at Ravelry.com has forums where you can post questions about specific yarns. Yarns come and go so quickly these days and there are so many beautiful yarns available.